T0399984

Developing Secure Attachment Through Play

Developing Secure Attachment Through Play offers a range of imaginative and engaging play-based activities, designed to help vulnerable young children forge safe attachments with their caregivers.

The book focuses on key developmental stages that may have been missed due to challenging life circumstances, such as social-emotional development, object permanence and physical and sensory development. It also considers pertinent issues including trauma, separation, loss and transition. Chapters explore each topic from a theoretical perspective, before offering case studies that illustrate the theory in practice, and a range of activities to demonstrate the effectiveness of play in developing healthy attachments.

Key features of this book include:

- 80 activities that can be carried out at home or in educational settings, designed to facilitate attachment and enhance social-emotional development;

- case vignettes exploring creative activities such as mirroring, construction play, physical play, baby doll play and messy play;

- scripts and strategies to create a safe and respectful environment for vulnerable children;

- photocopiable and downloadable resources, including early learning goals, a collection of therapeutic stories and a transition calendar.

By engaging children in these activities, parents, caregivers and practitioners can help the children in their care gain a sense of belonging and develop their self-esteem. This will be a valuable resource for early years practitioners, adoptive, foster and kinship parents, and therapists and social workers supporting young children.

Joan E. Moore is an author, drama therapist, play therapist and adoption support provider with foster, adoptive and kinship families. She works mainly with families in their home, applying her 'Theatre of Attachment' model of life history therapy. Joan has written several books and peer-reviewed articles. Her doctoral study at Leeds Beckett University on using story and drama to support these placements is described in *Narrative and Dramatic Approaches to Children's Life Story with Foster, Adoptive and Kinship Families*, published by Routledge. She supervises creative arts therapists and delivers training. Having a background in social work with children and families and youth justice, Joan has undertaken expert witness assessments of siblings, children's care needs, parents, and assessments of prospective adoptive parents, foster carers and kinship carers.

This is a definite 'must read' book, the latest from highly experienced therapist, Dr Joan Moore. It provides a wealth of practical ideas with underlying theory, and within the framework of Early Learning Goals. It will be an essential resource for parents and caregivers, especially for foster and adoptive parents, also for social workers, practitioners in care and education and all therapists addressing the developmental needs of children with attachment issues.

Dr Sue Jennings, Play and Dramatherapist, Neuro-Dramatic-Play LTD

Developing Secure Attachment Through Play

Helping Vulnerable Children Build their Social and Emotional Wellbeing

Joan E. Moore

Routledge
Taylor & Francis Group

LONDON AND NEW YORK

First published 2022
by Routledge
2 Park Square, Milton Park, Abingdon, Oxon OX14 4RN

and by Routledge
605 Third Avenue, New York, NY 10158

Routledge is an imprint of the Taylor & Francis Group, an informa business

British Library Cataloguing-in-Publication Data
A catalogue record for this book is available from the British Library

Library of Congress Cataloging-in-Publication Data
A catalog record has been requested for this book

ISBN: 978-0-367-71287-7 (hbk)
ISBN: 978-0-367-71288-4 (pbk)
ISBN: 978-1-003-15017-6 (ebk)

DOI: 10.4324/9781003150176

Typeset in Din Pro
by Newgen Publishing UK

Access the companion website: www.routledge.com/cw/speechmark

Contents

Foreword

'Just playing...' It is indisputable that from the very earliest age, play is a vitally important component to a child's overall development, learning and outcomes, not just in a physical sense, but cognitively, imaginatively, creatively, emotionally and socially. Successful development results from the experiences that children have through contact with others, which have far reaching impacts on their wellbeing and future development. The significance of these early experiences cannot be underestimated.

Play is the main way in which children learn about themselves and others, make sense of their experiences and express their emotions and their impulses to explore, experiment and understand. It is a means to developing key life skills and to learning about and building vital relationships.

As human babies we are born very physically underdeveloped, and our rate of development is slow compared to any other animal. We need more contact, touch, care and attention devoted to us for a hugely extended period, since we are so comparatively fragile, delicate, helpless and vulnerable during our early years. Paradoxically these are also the years of maximum opportunity, as well as maximum damage.

When these early experiences are positive, they provide a vital source of communication, connection, touch, and proximity and they promote a tolerance for these experiences with others. Supportive, nurturing adults create psychologically healthy children and young people. So far this is about when things go well enough.

For many children, sadly this is not their reality. Children who are 'looked after', not living in their 'birth family', but often in multiple households during childhood, or who have experienced neglect and trauma, are most likely to have missed these critical experiences and consequently are more likely to fail to achieve key stages of development to enable them to engage and progress, affecting their long-term life chances.

Changes in children's play over a single generation, as a consequence of contemporary culture, the development of technology, increased parental stress and anxiety, have placed restrictions on children's play opportunities, activities and experiences.

Foreword

Today in 2020, we have the additional negative impacts of the COVID-19 pandemic, with all the consequent anxieties, financial pressures and insecurities, isolation issues and implications for mental health and wellbeing. These all potentially impact on parents' and carers' capacity to meet their children's emotional needs, one of which is for play, as recognised in Article 31 of the United Nations Convention of the Rights of the Child.

For many children today, the COVID-19 pandemic has further reduced opportunities for social interaction and naturally occurring play experiences, from making meaning out of experiences through simple cause and effect, to more complex imaginary play scenarios. There are many potential long-term consequences from this, including the lack of opportunity for rehearsal, curiosity and exploration, to be able to work through frustrations and challenges and to express feelings in an emotionally secure environment.

The importance of intervening as early as possible in children's lives is well documented. The wellbeing of all children is a paramount social issue. It is everyone's responsibility to make homes, schools and communities responsive environments where children and young people can play, learn, achieve, feel safe and content.

Dr Joan Moore's breadth of skills, knowledge and understanding, drawn from a background in social work, adoption, play therapy and drama therapy, in addition to her research into the impacts of loss, trauma and disrupted attachments on children's development, have culminated in her 'Theatre of Attachment' model.

For anyone involved in this vital area, this latest text, *Developing Secure Attachment Through Play*, has an integrative role in connecting a broad range of elements including relationships, interaction, neuropsychology, mind and body through the experience of play. It will enable parents, carers, practitioners and students to incorporate new knowledge and theory into their interactions with children. This is not just about what children gain from nurturing play but what both children and adults can learn from the play experience that is reciprocal and relational.

Dr Joan Moore skilfully and succinctly identifies the significance of children's play and the emotional needs which are satisfied by play at each stage of development, and highlights relevant activities for each Early Learning Goal. She links theory with practice through a realistic approach and practical, achievable activities.

For anyone seeking a more meaningful and attuned connection with children, whatever your role, this book contains a wealth of practical solutions. It is a valuable resource for any parent or carer who wants to build a more interactive, playful and sensitive relationship with a child, and most significantly for those children who have missed early key emotional and developmental experiences, and where experiences have been chaotic, traumatic and unsafe.

For professionals supporting the parents and carers of these children, as well as for the parents and carers themselves, this book provides a clear structure, ensuring adults feel confident in their role in planning and engaging in play activities.

The resulting increased resilience, enjoyment, connection, sense of belonging and identity, confidence, communication and the opportunity for children to have some sense of control over their experiences, can motivate learning and enable the most vulnerable children to have an increased enjoyment in and understanding of themselves, others and their world.

I hope you all enjoy what this book has to offer, and I only wish I had had such a rich, accessible and valuable resource available to me at the beginning of my journey into the world of disadvantaged children and the complex challenges they face.

Linda Hoggan

Experienced manager in specialist assessment and early intervention services
Co-author with Carmen Kane of 'Just What We Need' therapeutic programme

Acknowledgements

Firstly, I would like to thank the parents and children, including those in foster, adoptive and kinship families, who inspired me to write this book. I have taken care to protect their confidentiality and to be sensitive to cultural issues. Many thanks to the social workers advocating for and supporting this intervention.

I am immensely grateful to Linda Hoggan for her generosity in writing the Foreword to this book. As 'Human Givens' psychotherapist, author and trainer of the therapeutic programme, 'Just What We Need', Linda has had many years' experience in early intervention, and particularly with traumatised children. I am also hugely grateful to Professor Sue Jennings, international author and trainer, for her valued endorsement. I am indebted to my gifted colleague Fran Taylor, art therapist, for all her wonderful illustrations. Also huge thanks to Rachel Stott, adoptive parent; Stacey Staples, early years teacher and manager; and Anne Healey, retired head teacher, for their insightful feedback.

Huge thanks also to Clare Ashworth, Senior Editor at Speechmark, and the publishing team at Routledge, for their faith in this book. Last but not least, I thank my husband, children, extended family and my friends for their enduring love and encouragement.

Introduction

This theory and practice book is for parents and caregivers seeking to enhance their relationship with young children and practitioners who are educating and supporting the children. It is particularly aimed at children who have missed key stages of development consequent to trauma, illness, loss or prematurity. It comes at a time of unprecedented circumstances caused by the COVID-19 pandemic and the lockdowns imposed to reduce its spread. The requirement of social distancing and hand sanitising alongside the prolonged closure of facilities has changed the course of human interaction and enforced new ways of being. Sigley (2020) points out that the necessity of having to suppress our senses and cut ourselves off from our support structures has led to the absence of tactile expression and this limits our ability to fully express empathy. The outcome of the first three months of lockdown has widened inequalities across age and gender in mental health as well as exacerbating existing inequalities (Banks and Xu, 2020).

Furthermore, the closure and restricted opening of early years provision has compromised vulnerable children's social, emotional, language and physical development. Being restricted to staying indoors with parents, many of whom have and are continuing to suffer from financial and other forms of stress combined with drastically reduced social contact, left young distressed children with no voice to alert others to their plight. Indeed Townsend (2020) reported an increase of 700% in calls to a helpline for victims of domestic violence. Fortunately, school and nursery provision have reopened. However, Pascal et al (2020) report an increase in risk for isolated young children, who having not been in regular contact with service providers, developed post-traumatic stress disorder (PTSD, see Glossary), attachment problems and a sense of grief, with long-term effects. At some stage, if and when the coronavirus is eradicated, children may have to relearn how to tolerate touch and relate to others in the pre-COVID (human) way. It will be best achieved through play since this is the means by which children communicate most naturally. Play does not come easily to all of us but this book will show how easy it can be and how effectively it can empower even distressed children such as those in the following sample of case vignettes:

The need for help in the early years

The UK care system has around 78,000 children at any one time (Department for Education [DfE], 2020). Many return to their parents and some receive additional support. Others remain in care and around 5% are placed for adoption for which the average age is just over four years. Faulconbridge et al (2018) find that investment in early help is associated with stronger outcomes for children.

Aimed at parents, caregivers, early years practitioners, teachers, classroom assistants, therapists and psychologists, each chapter of this book refers to the afore-mentioned children and many more to illustrate ways to nurture the children and bring on their development. Helping children learn to trust, attach securely and reach higher stages of learning is achieved through play activities with the active involvement of the adult. Play therapy (see Glossary) is of course a skill that requires professional training. This book is not a replacement for therapy but an addition to it. Play is the first step for children to get to know themselves and others. It is an opportunity to practice how to 'be' in real life within the privacy of it being not 'real'. As such, play is an effective way for parents and practitioners to communicate with children and better understand their perspective. Children learn by leading their own play and taking part in play that is guided by adults.

Early Learning Goals (Department for Education, 2020) are those defined by the government as relating to the prime areas of learning, i.e. communication and language, physical development, personal, social and emotional development. They include learning literacy, mathematics, and understanding the world, and also the goals of effective learning through playing and exploring, active learning and thinking critically. Appendix 1 is a chart of the Early Learning Goals. This is to enable early learning practitioners to identify the goals being met by the activities in which they engage the child. The cumulative effect of carrying out these activities and recording the date of their completion will enable parents, caregivers and early years practitioners (ELPs) to show when this is achieved and for ELPs to provide evidence of best practice. The activities can be used in various settings including the child's home, pre-school, school, family centres and clinical settings according to need.

Personal, social and emotional development is a prime area on which the government's statutory framework for early years (DfE, 2020) advises that children be helped:

> [t]o develop a positive sense of themselves, and others; to form positive relationships and develop respect for others; to develop social skills and learn how to manage their

feelings; to understand appropriate behaviour in groups; and to have confidence in their own abilities.

Early years practitioners are expected to be familiar with the different ways in which children learn and to reflect on these in their practice. Characteristics of effective teaching and learning are identified as allowing children to:

- play and explore – investigate, experience things and 'have a go';
- actively learn – concentrate, and if they encounter difficulties, to keep trying in order that they will be able to enjoy their achievements;
- create and think critically – develop their own ideas, make links between these ideas and develop strategies for doing things.

Early learning goals

The prime areas of learning and development in pre-school provision are summarised as follows:

Communication and Language Development

Developing children's skills at listening and attention, understanding and speaking, in order that they are able to follow instructions and stories, be receptive to others and develop their own stories.

Physical Development

Developing coordination, control and movement, via moving, negotiating space and handling equipment such as pencils and paint brushes; health and self-care, which includes helping children to recognise the benefits of a healthy diet, learn hygiene, dress themselves and use the toilet.

Personal, Social and Emotional Development

Building children's self-awareness and self-confidence to try new activities and talk about themselves, manage their feelings and behaviour, follow rules, make relationships, take turns in groups and be sensitive to others. Imaginative play activities help children to develop the specific learning areas of literacy and books. Play can incorporate activities such as counting and negotiating prices, which helps develop mathematical skills."

Understanding the World

Helping children to make sense of their environment, the key people in their past and present life, to understand similarities and differences in this as well as in places, objects and living things. This includes using technology, arts and crafts, incorporating a wide range of media for self-expression and exploration; also enabling children to learn to share their thoughts, ideas and feelings through activities such as music, movement, dance, role-play, and storytelling for developing their imagination.

How to use this book

While the book focuses primarily on early years development for children under five years, the activities are also suitable for older children whose development has been delayed for various reasons. Some activities such as those in Chapter 10 are particularly designed to meet the needs of older children and can be used at almost any stage up to and sometimes including adolescence. The reader is guided to study the following lists to decide what might be impeding the child, then turn to the relevant chapter for activities to address the issue and enable the child to catch up on this aspect of their development. The activities can be used in a variety of settings, such as in the child's home, educational settings (pre-school and school), family centres and clinical settings.

Notice the child's emotional age

Caregivers (foster, kinship, adoptive parents and early years professionals) will often appreciate that the distressed child is likely to be functioning at a younger emotional age, particularly when he or she feels stressed (hungry, upset or frustrated). The behaviour presented at these times may be years behind the child's chronological age and mirror the age at which they had their first separation from birth parents or the person with whom they felt safest.

Clues to recognising the child's emotional age:

(a) Timbre of the child's voice – does it sound higher or more whimpering than you would expect, given the child's actual age?

(b) Movements – for instance, hiding under furniture or behind doors and peeping out; crawling even though the child can walk perfectly well.

(c) Gait – for example, I have observed a neglected 12-year-old boy run around in the waddling manner of a two-year-old wearing a full nappy.

(d) Actions of biting and chewing – suggestive of age 6–9 months, the stage at which babies put everything in their mouths to see what it tastes like.

(e) Hitting, snatching and punching – the child who is delayed in sensory processing may be unaware of their strength or its effect because learning gaps will have affected their brain's ability to make connections. Or they may be simply emotionally frustrated from not feeling loved and cared for.

Consider what might be delaying the child's development

The reader is guided to study the following lists to decide what might be impeding the child then turn to the relevant chapter for activities to address the issue and enable the child to catch up on this aspect of their development.

Social and emotional development: Does the child show insecure patterns of relating, such as withdrawal and hiding; is the child being confrontational, taking extreme risks, or struggling to cope with separating from you? Does the child recognise the implicit social signals expected of their age? See Chapter 1.

Trauma: Does the child present as hypervigilant, perpetually on the alert and unable to focus for long on any task? Does the child have accidents of wetting and soiling? How often is the child tired? How well is the child sleeping? Is the child afraid to sleep or does she or he suffer nightmares or night terrors? See Chapter 2.

Mirroring (see Glossary): Does the child make eye contact easily? Is the child comfortable with being cuddled? Does the child show affection appropriately? See Chapter 3.

Object permanence (see Glossary): Does the child manage separation from caregivers? Does the child have adequate stimulation? Is the child encouraged to explore? Is the child nervous about trying new activities? Does the child show curiosity? Is the child excited or fearful on discovering things in play? See Chapter 4.

Cause and effect (see Glossary): Does the child show recognition of the consequences of their actions? Does the child understand the effect their behaviour has on others? Is the child accustomed to or reliant on having their play supervised? Does the child take lots of risks or avoid situations involving risk-taking? Can the child make friends? How does the child react to praise? Does the child believe it? See Chapter 5.

Physical development: Can the child climb stairs, jump and move without tripping on things? Does he or she show fear of particular foods or of being poisoned? Does the child seem excessively hungry (possibly due to a history of irregular and unpredictable feeds)? See Chapter 6.

Language development: Does the child understand what you say to him or her? Does he/she make sounds unusual for his/her age? Does the child fail to pay attention to explanations? Does the child struggle socially? See Chapter 7.

Separation and loss: Has the child undergone many changes of care? Does he or she appear to be grieving the loss of a parent? Is he or she struggling to trust or bond (see Glossary) with new parents or caregivers? Will he or she seem to 'go to anyone' regardless of how well he or she knows the person? See Chapter 8.

Managing transition: Is the child able to cope satisfactorily with transitions?

Does she/he show anxiety about going to school or coming home? If the child has had several changes of care, does he/she worry who is collecting or will be looking after him/her at home, nursery, playgroup or school? See Chapter 9.

Identity Formation: Does the child have a positive sense of his/her identity and where he/she comes from (compared to their peers of the same age and ethnicity)? Does the child play appropriately? Does the child feel part of the family he or she lives with? See Chapter 10.

Contents of this book

The opening to each chapter briefly explains the theory in relation to the topic it covers. Key points are given to summarise the main points. This is followed by two case studies to illustrate the theory and ways in which early years practitioners, caregiving parents and therapists can engage the children, so as to clarify the context and purpose of the activities. Scripts and strategies follow the activities, to enable the reader to address particular predicaments.

Chapter 1 reflects on the impact of social and emotional delay on children's attachment (see Glossary) to their parents and caregivers. In the interests of building secure attachment and enhancing the children's ability to make friends, activities focus on how to reflect, name feelings, as well as nurture play.

Chapter 2 explains the impact of traumatic experience, reminders of which trigger children into a state of alarm, which impedes their ability to focus and self-regulate. It reflects on relational constraints, which could hinder the child's ability to trust in safe adults. Case studies demonstrate how trauma can be worked through in play. Suggestions are made for activities which can be carried out in a quiet space to facilitate this process so that the child is enabled to build a more secure attachment to his or her caregivers.

Chapter 3 focuses on the mirroring interaction which Hughes (2004, 2017) refers to as the 'attachment dance' that takes place between nurturing parents and their infants. This is an experience frequently missed by young children subjected to neglect, abuse and trauma. The proposed activities include mirroring, movement, vocal exercises, and other sensory experiences, to encourage heightened emotional reciprocity.

Chapter 4 explains the significance of 'object permanence' which is learned by nurtured children in the first year of life. Many vulnerable children, who lack the opportunity to safely explore their environment in early childhood, struggle later to cope with separation. The activities in this chapter will help them to overcome their fears through the safety of play. Children are enabled to practice the predicaments that they may otherwise struggle to navigate.

Chapter 5 on 'cause and effect' describes how children learn about the effect they have on the people around them. The creative activities presented will encourage children to use the safe context of play to experiment at taking different roles, discover how much space their body movement takes up and through fictional privacy, learn about 'the domino effect' of consequences.

Chapter 6 on delay in physical development and sensory integration explains how to recognise particular problems facing the most vulnerable children. It details the neural systems affecting capacity for sensory integration. The play activities enable them to catch up on their development in these areas include games, use of trampolines, sand, water, junk-modelling and animal Olympics.

Chapter 7 on enabling language and speech development, explains the context, impact and warning signs of this aspect of delay in development. Activities aimed at addressing this delay include: dramatic play – tour of discovery; a Strictly Come Dancing game, sharing stories, naming songs, creative visualisation, telephone conversations and other games.

Chapter 8 focuses on the impact of separation and loss on young children, particularly those who have been parted from their parents of origin. The activities are designed to rebuild the children's attachment by helping them to understand the reasons for their situation in a way that explains without inferring blame. Various sensory and creative materials are proposed to enable the caregiving parents and practitioners to engage the children more effectively.

Chapter 9 illustrates the impact of transition for children, especially those in foster, kinship and adoptive families who have had multiple changes of care. To rebuild their future and help the children adapt to changes in their circumstances, proposed activities include the 'road of feelings' exercise, story bags, ways to use dolls houses, and clay modelling for storytelling.

Chapter 10 on identity reflects on cultural considerations and the context necessary for young children to build a positive identity. Case studies of older children show the consequences of negative identity formed from subjection to neglect and abuse. They illustrate the application of activities, scripts and strategies showing ways to rebuild children's self-esteem and self-image.

There are five **Appendices**. These include:

(1) a chart of Early Learning Goals for parents and caregivers to check which are met by the child's engagement in particular activities;

(2) play activities for stimulating imagination;

(3) a school day clock for use as a template to help children make links between clock time and associated activities;

(4) a transition calendar for children moving to a new foster or adoptive home;

(5) five stories to use alongside activities in the chapters applying the following steps: The parent or caregiver reads a story the child is likely to enjoy, and shows deep interest in their feelings. The parent or caregiver then invites the child to play with toys and or materials (sand, play dough, etc.) to create their own story, which the parent/caregiver praises. As the cycle repeats multiple times, the child is enabled to continue the creative process with less need of support from adults (Moore, 2020).

A **glossary of terms** is also provided to guide the reader who is unfamiliar with certain theoretical terms.

Meet the children

> *Georgia, aged 33 months, resisted all forms of restraint, be it car seatbelt, highchair, reins or her adoptive parents' attempts to hold and cuddle her. An angry child, she avoided eye contact and her tantrums lasted for hours.*

> *Conor, aged 4, was a 'frozen' unattached child, who would 'go to anyone', having frequently been left at home alone or in company of drug users. The foster carer experienced Conor to be controlling and attention seeking.*

> *Jessie, aged 4, ran into roads, regardless of danger. She vied for attention from complete strangers and persistently put herself at risk.*

> *Robbie, aged 2, took a long time to go up or down stairs. Being ignored and left for hours in a baby seat stuck between two armchairs had affected his vision and delayed his language and physical development.*

> *Amela, aged 4, experienced being taken to her adoptive family as 'kidnap'. Showing no recognition of their authority, she spoke to them as her peers.*

> *Danny, aged 4, didn't understand why he'd been taken to live with his new parents. He was hyperactive and wrecked his toys. His poor speech and understanding left them worn out from endlessly repeating instructions.*

While the experience of looking after children can be highly rewarding, these and the other case examples illustrate the challenges for which caregiving parents, early years practitioners, social workers and clinicians, are often unprepared and at a loss to know how to address. The adult's best intentions to provide security and quality care can be thrown off-kilter by these children's fearful resistance to attaching securely. Frustrated by struggles to communicate, their challenging behaviour frequently compounds the problem. Traumatic reminders of not having their needs met for food, warmth, nurture, care and affection are bound to reactivate their stress responses.

The Department for Education recognise the significance that personal, emotional and social education has for achievement and wellbeing. According to Ofsted (DfE, 2020), 55.9% of looked after children had a special educational need compared with 46% of 'children in need' and 14.9% of all children. For children requiring specialist support, social, emotional and mental health are the most common types of help needed by those in care and adopted. Many will have been affected by their parents' inability to cope due to mental ill health, learning difficulties, aggressive parenting, substance abuse and violence. In such predicaments, children all too frequently miss out on key stages of development. This in turn affects their expectations of relationships. A key finding from a longitudinal study by Caspi et al (2016) is that the futures of the study children could be predicted at three years of age. The study found that 22% of the segment involved multiple high costs to the country's economy (78% prescription fills and 81% criminal convictions). For this group the main factors were: growing up in a socially deprived family, exposure to maltreatment, low IQ and poor self-control, yet risks could be ameliorated through early years support.

The UK government requires all areas of learning and development in the early years to be implemented through planned, purposeful play and a mix of adult-led and child-initiated activity. Play is acknowledged as being essential for development and for building confidence while children are learning to explore, think about problems and relate to others. Play is found to increase production of neuropeptides – oxytocin, dopamine and serotonin, the brain chemicals which enhance wellbeing, and as Music (2014) points out, help to insulate the brain from anxiety and depression. This is particularly significant for children suffering trauma, neglect and abuse.

Trauma

Life can be very stressful for all sorts of reasons – illness, disease, poverty, unemployment, divorce and loss of important relationships. For the most vulnerable children, trauma affects the capacity to learn and relate to others. Many children in foster, kinship care or who are adopted have experienced hostility and depression from their birth parents, who themselves are traumatised. Gerhardt (2004) explains that if children are feeling threatened, their stress response system can activate over prolonged periods. Unfortunately, in the arena of child and family practice, less research has been carried out on younger children, especially the youngest age group. Child abuse enquiries have found that reliance on parents' accounts and discounting what the verbal child expresses has led to severe errors of judgement (Bunston and Jones, 2020: 31).

Jenney (2020: 93) found mothers with a trauma history were often frightened by their child's tantrums and sensed a need to protect themselves from the child. They believe these behaviours – tantrums and separation anxiety, which are normal developmental stages – are somehow malevolent or dangerous. Fear prevents traumatised parents from feeling able to contain their child's distress. In research on mothers with PTSD, Schechter et al (2008) found the more severe the mother's trauma was, the more distance she kept from her child. It is easy to see how legacies of early neglect and abuse compromise children's ability to sustain healthy friendships and relationships. However, it makes the task of helping them to achieve these goals especially challenging.

The DfE statutory framework has recognised that lack of stimulation and social deprivation during early childhood lead to a variety of developmental problems including language delay, fine and gross motor delays, impulsivity, dysphoria, disorganised attachment, attention difficulties and hyperactivity. As Selwyn et al (2014), Perry et al (2006) and Perry (2002) have noted, poor cognitive development and language delay hamper the child's progress in school. Naughton et al, (2013) saw neglected infants and toddlers show a dramatic decline in their overall developmental scores between the ages of 9 months and 24 months.

Brandon et al (2014: 8) describe the physical impact of neglect on the brain:

Exposure to neglect, often alongside other forms of maltreatment, is associated with alterations in the development of the hypothalamic-pituitary-adrenal (HPA) axis stress response and differences in brain structure and function.

The authors add that fortunately, there is 'considerable evidence to suggest that many neglected children who are placed away from home in foster care or with adoptive families can catch up on developmental deficits'.

Lyndsey and Dockerell's review (2012: 4) *The Better Communication Research Programme*, was commissioned by the Department of Education in response to the Bercow (2008) review of services for children and young people with speech, language and communication needs. Bercow had recommended a programme of research 'to enhance the evidence base and inform delivery of better outcomes for children and young people' (p.50). Lyndsey and Dockerell warn that children and young people with speech, language and communication needs and those on the autistic spectrum are at increased risk of developing behavioural, emotional and social difficulties although there are different patterns for different domains.Overall, the main areas of difficulty are with the development of successful peer relationships and pro-social behaviour, and the risk of developing emotional difficulties. All of these start in the early years.

Children attach to their parents because they need to be looked after. Those accustomed to rejecting and unpredictable responses adapt their behaviour by becoming more demanding (crying harder) or withdrawing in the hope that avoiding attention will ensure their safety. If, regardless of the child's efforts, their needs continue to be unmet, it is likely that their attachment behaviour will become disorganised and maladaptive. The child continues to expect rejection even after being taken to a nurturing environment. The impact on the subsequent caregivers, who become worn down by the children's rejecting behaviour, requires a creative approach that helps these children grow to trust their caregivers and develop mutually rewarding relationships. Play is integral to the process of improving relationships with the children. Even though attitudes to play vary across different cultures, children need to feel they are special to their parents as well as fully supported and loved by them.

Delay in development

Bunston and Jones (2020: 38) emphasise that it is 'imperative to provide a rapid and flexible response' since the longer children are left in states of dysregulation, the more lasting the damage will be to their brains. Educational theorists such as Piaget and Vygotsky, and contemporary findings in neuroscience (see Glossary) have demonstrated that the brain (and the capacity to understand) develops mainly sequentially in identified stages. So, to ensure the efficacy of attempts to help children we must take their level of functioning into account. For instance, it is pointless to expect an infant to stop crying on request, or a two-year-old to understand feelings expected of a child aged six or seven.

Neglected children will not have developed the same understanding of the world as their average peers. In fact, emotional delay leaves them less able to respond as expected of their actual age. For example, they may not say 'please' and 'thank you' or follow simple instructions. The child who has missed out on the experience of being held, talked to, comforted, admired and stimulated in play, or who has had their physical and emotional needs only partially met, is likely to have missed vital windows for development. Yet we know that once they are well nurtured, they usually progress to the higher stages of learning.

Touch and close proximity to others can raise anxiety in traumatised children. The fear of coronavirus and the requirement to maintain social distance can only exacerbate these anxieties. Play is the most natural way to mitigate it and help children build more healthy relationships based on trust. We all need to be able to 'self-regulate' in order to function successfully in a social group, to think logically and recognise others' feelings when they differ from our own. Play is the means by which children explore their world and relationships and practice ways of 'being'. Indeed Vygotsky (1978) identified the pre-school child's use of 'private speech' to talk to themselves in play and self-instruct as their first vehicle for voluntary self-regulation. Most pre-school children are not ready to consider the rights and views of others – they need external guidance, rules and constraints. Sensory reminders of past trauma can trigger memories which cause children to regress to the age at which a traumatic incident (such as separation from their birth parents) first happened. This can be at the stage that Piaget (1952) identified as 'pre-operational'. Therefore, caregivers who are seeking to develop a relationship with their children are advised to focus on the following specific areas.

- sensitivity/attunement (see Glossary) – use of eye contact, voice tone, pitch and rhythm, facial expression and touch to convey synchronicity;

- applying mind-mindedness and mentalisation (Fonagy and Target, 2006; see Glossary) – in other words, the capacity to experience the child as an intentional being with his or her own personality traits, strengths and sensitivities;

- mirror the child's affect (see Glossary) by making a contingent response, e.g. looking sad when the child is crying, but without becoming overwhelmed by it;

- using touch, gesture and speech to contain the child's powerful feelings;

- reciprocity (turn-taking) and consistency of care – provide young children with sufficient continuity of caretaking to enable secure attachment;

- Communicate with the child through play and story making (Moore, 2012, 2014, 2019, 2020). This will develop the child's imagination, creativity and problem solving abilities, thus propelling the child on the path to self-fulfilment and to reaching their potential for self-actualisation (Maslow, 1970).

The significance of stories and story making

Myths, fairy tales and nursery rhymes have long been used to entertain and engage young children in exploring ways to deal with feelings and situations. Children love make-believe. They easily identify with feelings expressed by the like of animals that 'talk'. Sharing the emotions aroused in this tantalising process brings joy – both from hearing stories and rhymes and from the process of creating their own. It enables children to learn about the effect their emotions and actions have on other people and how these people respond. Literature offers a magnificent range of characters, personalities, attributes and actions (Jennings, 2004). As Frude and Killick (2011) and Killick (2014) reflect, the listener is made privy to the inner world of characters' thought processes, which in turn enables the listener to discover their own. It is a process that enhances emotional literacy (Thomas and Killick, 2007) and mentalisation skills (Fonagy and Target, 2006) – the ability to listen and reflect sensitively.

The role of the adult in this process is highly significant. Caregivers and parents can replicate the mother-infant 'attachment dance' (Hughes, 2004; Trevarthen, 2005) by amplifying their emotional response as they engage with joyful emotions and demonstrate control of their negative emotions. The child models on the adult and learns to self-soothe and to feel hope. At the anxiety-inducing moment in a story when the fictional hero (let's say a 'mermaid') is in the clutches of a 'villain', the parent might say, *'Ooh! How scary! Shall we turn the page over and see if someone rescues the mermaid?'* This helps the child, who identifies with the hero's plight, both to contain her anxiety and to anticipate rescue. Stories lend the distance that makes it easier to deal with scary feelings and situations which in real life threaten to overwhelm.

The structure of nursery rhymes and stories invite gleeful repetition of familiar lines such as *'I'll huff and I'll puff and I'll blow your house down'* which prepare the listener for what will happen next. The creative process of story-making and the accompanying activities provide a 'transitional space' (Winnicott, 1971) for witnessing actions and reactions. It is therefore important to provide children in the early years with activities that will stimulate lively interactions and encourage their development. This will help them to establish and maintain a more secure attachment to nurturing parents and caregivers.

1 Social and emotional development

Introduction

Neuroscience provides increasing evidence of the damage that emotional neglect causes to children's social and emotional development. Music (2020: 9) refers to research showing that the consequences are often 'far more devastating than overt trauma on brains, psyches and relationship capacities'. As the eminent late child psychiatrist John Bowlby (2007) explained, children's fear of not having their needs met leads them to 'retreat from the world' (to avoid upsetting scary parents) or 'do battle with it' (to keep the distracted parent's attention). The child's instinct is to try every measure to ensure their survival. How children experience caregiving in the early years therefore profoundly affects their capacity to be in satisfying relationships.

Explaining attachment

Attachment theory was developed by Bowlby and concerns children's need for safety and security in their relationships with their parents and caregivers. It is a model for understanding the bewildering, sometimes anti-social behaviour of insecure children, who experience painful early separation and loss of important relationships consequent to neglect and abuse. Securely attached children self-regulate, show empathy, seek help when they need it and adjust more quickly after threats and upsets. Their belief in their right to be in the world contrasts with that of insecurely attached children, who do not share this conviction and instead can be highly anxious but not always show it. The insecure child might seem avoidant and dismissive, or may be especially clingy, perpetually seeking reassurance. If we recognise these patterns of interaction it becomes easier to meet the children's needs by giving them the reassurance and nurture they need. Through the safety of play, we can enable them to practice new, healthier ways of meeting the world and enjoying the company of others.

Learning empathy

To enjoy reciprocal relationships requires the capacity for empathy (see glossary) and compassion. We learn this from having our emotional states reflected back to us by our parents. The process starts with the mirroring interactions between parents and infants as described in Chapter 3. This is often referred to as the 'attachment dance' (Hughes, 2004), which involves the parent echoing and amplifying the baby's vocalisations. As the 'dance' repeats multiple times, the baby learns of the parent's deep interest in them and accordingly is reassured. Babies learn to smile reciprocally within a few weeks of birth, although babies of highly anxious mothers smile less because their mothers smile less. By 12 months, infants can distinguish between different expressions and begin to understand that other people have intentions. They start to 'pretend' (to feed dolly) and imitate parent's behaviours (such as 'vacuuming', using a push along toy). From around 18 months, nurtured toddlers begin to show ability to respond sensitively to others' feelings as they develop 'theory of mind' – the realisation that others may think differently to them (Baron-Cohen et al, 1985).

All children rely on their parents to be role models and leaders, who organise things for them for as long as this is needed. However, parents have many responsibilities, which include keeping their children safe and teaching them social rules. Therefore, from the moment young children become mobile, they hear the word 'No' said to them repeatedly. Schore (2006) found this word being issued approximately every nine minutes of the young child's waking hours. Such prohibitions have the effect of shaming the child into submission. Of course, children need to be kept safe and need to learn that certain behaviours, such as picking their nose and pinching people, are not welcomed. However, when shame is too prolonged it becomes toxic.

Sensitive parents counter its impact by quickly re-attuning, giving the child explanations and reassurance: *I don't want you to hurt yourself, I love you too much!* However, parents who have not experienced much sensitivity or nurturing in their childhoods are likely to be far less intuitive in this respect. They may not think of issuing the reassurance their child needs. The child raised in an emotionally negative or hostile environment comes to expect people to be unkind and mean. His ability to tolerate his own and others' feelings relates to his capacity to bear pain. The most far-reaching effect of neglect and trauma is the inability to self-calm when he is feeling anxious.

Key messages

- Notice patterns being repeated in the play.

- Allow the child's expression of negative and positive emotions.

- Echoing the child's phrases emulates the attachment dance.

Case examples
Steven, aged 3

The parents of Steven and his brother squabbled and fought so much they were unable to think about what their children needed. Their father was sent to prison after which their mother died in a house fire. The boys were placed in foster care, but in different homes due to Steven's brother's special needs. Social workers identified an adoptive family for Steven, who was being prepared to meet them. Having already lost his parents and been separated from his brother, Steven was about to experience the loss of his foster family with whom he had built his first trusting relationship. His behaviour alternated between running off and hiding, and demanding attention. Going between the two extremes indicated a pattern of disorganised attachment, whereby the betrayed child does not know how to go about getting his needs met. Play helped Steven make a safe transition to adoption. In the play kitchen he saw (toy) knives and immediately announced, *'This is a dangerous place!'*

HOW STEVEN'S FOSTER PARENT HELPED

Steven's stories featured fires, which he insisted could never be put out. He buried toy people in sand to keep them safe from anticipated scary predators. Steven was offered a calming activity of making pictures with collage materials. Alighting on a bag of pasta shapes, he shook out the pieces of pasta and covered them in multiple layers of sticky plastic. Then, on finding the dressing up bag, he adorned himself in layer upon layer of clothing. This process of layering appeared to be Steven's way of expressing his need for protection (from harm as well as the cold), unconsciously. In puppet play, his characters were repeatedly heard saying, *'I've had enough of you!'* – a phrase that Steven had often heard said to him. Permission to express his rage and frustration in the safety of the play context enabled him to attach to his new parents. Steven settled satisfactorily in his adoptive family.

Carly, aged 4

Carly had multiple episodes in foster care between being returned to her mother from whom she was eventually removed permanently. A plan was made for adoption. Her early years practitioner (ELP) tried to prepare Carly for this move and realised Carly was feeling unsafe. In one-to-one play, she engaged Carly in a game of Pass the Parcel with dolls but Carly's manner was flat, expressing how powerless she felt being passed from one caregiver to another. She took her characters on a journey in a carriage that in her words kept 'shaking you up'. The central character didn't know where she was going and why. Carly proceeded to bury (toy) people in sand to protect them from a scary creature threatening to 'come and get them'. These buried people were then abandoned, their plight unrecognised. Anyone who tried to escape was caught, tied up and held captive (echoing Carly's past experience).

HOW THE ELP HELPED CARLY

On seeing dolls of different sizes Carly was enticed to experiment at how she might grow up to be a 'big girl'. Entranced by the doll's house, she set up scenes in each of the rooms. She had the dolls watch various programmes on the (toy) television and make 'telephone calls' to arrange social get-togethers. Carly appeared to be exploring the social roles and mores, which she sensed would be expected of her when she moved into her adoptive placement.

Activities

The following activities will enable parents and early years practitioners to emulate the playful mother-infant relationship – the 'attachment dance' – that most neglected children typically miss in their early infancy.

Feelings chart

Make up a chart of happy, sad and angry faces – there are plenty of these charts online. Add symbols to illustrate feelings – such as tears to show sadness; heart for 'love'; storm cloud for 'worry' and a jagged mouth to express 'anger'.

Invite the child to point to the chart and show you which face matches his or her feeling. This can be done before the guided play session and at the end, as a means of enabling the child to show you if and how their feeling changed.

EARLY LEARNING GOALS

ELG01: Listening and attention – in mirror play the child learns to listen, anticipate what the adult will do next, and respond with the same actions.

ELG03: Speaking – children learn to express themselves, develop their own narratives and explanations and connect ideas.

ELG08: Self-confidence and self-awareness – this is gained from learning to follow rules, cooperate and be sensitive to others.

Shop play

Items needed for playing 'shops' are easily substituted. For example, if you don't have a till, a shoebox will suffice. Cut out 'bank cards' and 'bank notes' from card and leaflets and use buttons as 'coins'. Children continue to be fascinated by coins and notes. Play credit cards can also be incorporated. This play serves as a way for children to practice negotiating skills with different personalities, and conflict situations. Provide a few tins and packets, dusters, washing up liquid, etc. Pictures of goods can also be cut out from leaflets and pasted onto card to represent the 'goods' on sale.

The child can act as the 'till lady' and serve the 'customers'. The adult takes the role of various customers – a role the child can also take turns at. The 'customer' might, for example, be a window cleaner, park keeper, train driver, doctor, farmer, librarian, astronaut, clown, footballer, ballet dancer, or scientist. Encourage the child to develop a story about what happens next. Check whether she would like you to be a 'nice' or a 'naughty' customer. If she suggests 'naughty' the customer might 'run out of money and take an item without paying for it'. Talk to the child about why the customer would do this. Decide what happens next. Will she be given another chance or not?

Use the privacy of the fictional role to explain people's behaviour, views and assumptions. The story being about 'someone else' protects the child's privacy. It is important to use words and phrases the child recognises and to check that she has understood your explanations. Giving patient responses to children's repeated questions will demonstrate your interest and genuine enthusiasm for playing with them. Also, praising children for their ideas will help them learn from the experience in play and raise their self-esteem.

EARLY LEARNING GOALS

ELG03: Speaking – children learn to express themselves. They develop their own narratives and explanations and connect ideas.

ELG08: Making relationships – shop play gives children practice at taking turns, trying out roles and ways of being in relationship with others.

ELG12: Shape, space and measures – in shop play, children learn about shapes, space and measures, concepts of size, weight, capacity, position, distance, time and money; they also compare quantities and objects.

ELG16: Exploring and using media and materials – this form of play enables children to learn life skills such as counting (change), making choices and thinking about other people's needs.

Painting landscapes and seascapes

Painting stimulates imagination and can lead into story making about the scene painted. Provide card, jars half filled with water (to hold brushes), water-soluble paint and brushes of comfortable length for the child to hold. Painting landscapes and seascapes is mainly for older children but some four-year-olds are capable of this, while younger ones can do their own version and will tell you what they have drawn even if it is not easily recognisable.

LANDSCAPES

Invite the child to paint a picture of a beautiful place. Sit alongside to paint with him if he needs this encouragement. The avoidant child might produce a landscape empty of features. Suggest he adds a person or animal to his picture. Then ask if this character needs a friend to be with. Point out that adventures are more fun if you have someone to share them with. Let's imagine the child draws a dog. The dog might need shelter – a house or tree.

Ask the child about the weather in this scene – is it raining or sunny? Perhaps the child has drawn a bird in the sky and a dog by the tree. The bird could say what it sees or the dog be given a bone. To invite story making, you might wonder what happens next. Invite the child to make a clay or play dough model of figures in his painting. With the models he can enact the story and plan the outcome. Show approval of his efforts, however immature they are.

SEASCAPES

Begin by telling the story, *The Star that Lost its Shine* (Appendix 5, Story 4). Invite the child to paint a picture of it. Ask her if the weather in her picture will be stormy or calm and sunny. Distressed children may choose a 'stormy' scene. This may mirror the atmosphere that has been familiar to them. Consider whether it is day or night – light or dark? Are there stars in the sky? Suggest adding a boat to the picture. Ask if someone will be in the boat. Perhaps a fisherman comes to the rescue. This story might be dramatised or a new one told.

EARLY LEARNING GOALS

ELG16: Exploring and using media and materials – enables experimentation.

ELG17: Using imagination – children share their thoughts, feelings, imagination, ideas and create stories from their paintings.

Islands

Start by telling a story about three islands, the first is an island that has everything desirable on it – trees, shelter, food, kind people, sunshine etc. The second island is an island of waiting (to get to the desirable island). The third island is a place of danger, sadness, coldness and emptiness. Suggest to the

child that you will help them make these islands and see how you can get from one to the other and what might happen on each one.Islands can be built from equipment such as floor cushions and pieces of coloured fabric to 'be' the 'beach' 'sea', 'rocks' or 'volcanoes'.

The 'island' could be painted on large paper. Add features and arrange items such as trees and houses to be stuck onto the island picture.

Alternatively, construct an island from play dough, air-drying modelling clay, or paper mâché (torn strips of kitchen paper dipped in a thin paste with PVA glue and water). Spread strips of soaked paper over moulded newspaper, a balloon or dried clay. Use pipe cleaners and tissue paper, play dough or clay to make people and animals. Have a few small boxes to construct houses or shelters like barns.

Talk to the child about what is on each of the islands. What does it look like from each side? Is there a house or volcano? Is it safe? Who lives there? Are there islands nearby? Is it an island of plenty with trees and food – or an island of emptiness, featureless and bleak? Can boats travel between the islands? Draw and take photos of the island. Develop the story about the islands.

EARLY LEARNING GOALS

ELG14: The world – this activity enables the child to recognise similarities and differences in places, objects, materials and living things; also, to make comparisons with the features of their immediate environment. Children's observations of people, animals and plants will help them to explain why some things happen, and how things change.

Story-making with bricks or buttons

Have a collection of Duplo or Lego bricks to use for 'scenery', such as houses, fire station, etc. Buttons can be used to represent 'people'. These materials stimulate the imagination and serve to create all sorts of backdrops.

Help the child to create a scene such as: School, home, park, soft play area, shop, swimming pool, party, cinema, zoo, beach, mountains, forest,

launderette, garage, circus, outer space, office, castle, safari park, hospital, hairdressers, dentist, vets' practice, etc.

Allow the child to lead the play, but have a few ideas ready in case he or she lacks confidence to take the play forward. Showing interest in children's ideas and following their lead will convey how important they are to you. It will help them to feel more confident and to attach more securely to safe caregivers.

EARLY LEARNING GOALS

ELG01: Listening and attention – in this play, children will listen and attend.

ELG02: Understanding – children gain more understanding of others.

ELG03: Speaking – children express their ideas and cooperate with others.

ELG06: Self-confidence and self-awareness – increases as children develop their narratives and begin to sensitively take on others' ideas.

ELG12: Shape, space and measures – using Duplo bricks helps children to learn about proportions and how things fit together, and to connect ideas.

ELG14: The world – children learn to recognise similarities and differences in relation to places, objects and materials as they compare environments.

ELG17: Explaining by connecting ideas – from engaging in imaginative play in various settings, children make observations of people and animals, which enable them to explain why some things happen, and how they change.

Bad dreams

Many vulnerable children will have experienced trauma causing upsetting dreams. In these dreams, their mind plays out fears, but while the child is sleeping, he is not in control of what seems to be happening to him. Nightmares may feature multi-sensory images, sounds, smells, textures and interactions. Nightmares and night terrors can feel truly terrifying for the child and cause him to wet or soil the bed. He may be too scared to go to sleep, dreading the dream he expects to plague him as soon as he loses consciousness. Trying to stay awake will leave the child exhausted during

the day. Yet he may be too scared to tell anyone about the dream in case doing so makes it even more real. Suggest to the child that a favourite doll or teddy will listen to him if he tells it his scary dream. Listen carefully, reassure the child and address his worry. Playing out the dream in the daytime helps to reduce its intensity for the child in the presence of a secure adult, who is saying, '*Look what that monster did! It was so mean!*'

EARLY LEARNING GOALS

ELG01: Listening and attention – the child models on the attentive adult.

ELG05: Health and self-care – children gain mastery over their fears. This activity helps them gain control over their personal needs, including toileting.

Draw the worry

On learning of a child's worries, encourage the child to draw pictures of them. You can write a label for each one. Then decide what to do with the worries. Some concerning the future can go into a special box for safekeeping. If the child's worry is about not being able to do a task set him in school or nursery the parent might give this worry to the child's teacher to help him know what to do. If it is about not being collected from pre-school, the early years practitioner can show the child a picture of the person due to collect him, or give him an item of the parents' to look after (see Strategies in Chapter 4). Children in care and adopted might have anxieties regarding contact with birth relatives. These worries need to be passed on to their social worker to answer queries. The children are then relieved of the worries that are the adult's responsibility.

EARLY LEARNING GOALS

ELG01: Listening and attention – the child models on the attentive adult.

ELG02: Understanding – hearing stories help children to connect to feelings.

ELG05: Health and self-care – children gain mastery over their fears. This activity helps them gain control over their personal needs, including toileting.

ELG07: Managing feelings and behaviour – in time, through exploring their ideas and beliefs children gain confidence in managing their feelings.

Decorate biscuits

Invite the child to ice and decorate biscuits. Icing biscuits is a nurturing activity. It can also be used alongside the activities described above for dealing with children's troubling dreams. Coloured decorating pens can be used to draw an image of the monster plaguing the child's dreams. As the child eats the biscuit, help her to believe that she is actually getting rid of the 'monster' that can't come back any more.

EARLY LEARNING GOALS

ELG01: Listening and attention – the child models on the attentive adult.

ELG05: Health and self-care – children gain mastery over their fears. This activity helps them gain control over their anxieties about sleeping.

Stories about worries

Children gain confidence on hearing stories, which illustrate ways of dealing with fears. Check the local library for books. Here are a few suggestions:

Scared of the Dark (Alexander, 1986) – a story in which scary sights such as 'snakes' under the character's bed turn out to be just a pair of socks.

The Very Noisy Night (Hendry and Chapman, 1999) – the story of a mouse, who, when helped by big brother, comes to realise the source of troubling noises and images, such as shadows, a wind blowing the curtains, etc. Eventually the mouse sleeps peacefully.

There's a Nightmare in my Cupboard (Mayer, 1991) – this is the story of a little boy finding a monster that turns out to be even more frightened than the boy.

EARLY LEARNING GOALS

ELG01: Listening and attention – the child models on the attentive adult.

ELG02: Understanding – stories enable children to connect to feelings.

ELG03: Speaking – children learn to express themselves effectively.

ELG05: Health and self-care – children gain mastery over their fears. This activity helps them gain control over their personal needs, including toileting.

ELG07: Managing feelings and behaviour – in time, as children explore their ideas and beliefs and develop stories in imaginative play, they will gain confidence for managing their feelings, behaviour and relationships.

Scripts and strategies
Model calmness

Children emulate the adults around them and will be affected by caregivers' stress. Demonstrate a calm thoughtful approach to stressful situations by having a list of tasks of manageable length to talk through with the child:

First we have breakfast and then we go to school. On the way back I'll go to the shops. At 3pm I'll come to school to take you home. Then you play, while I get the dinner ready. At 6pm you have a bath and at 7pm its time for bed.

Visual timetable

Simplifying the day's routine to the major points reduces the child's need to worry about every small part of it. Having a visual timetable with detachable photos or symbols for the child to post into a box when the routine has been accomplished allows the child to gain a sense of achievement (a bit like crossing things off a list) and see the pile reduce as 'home time' approaches.

Relaxation

Encourage the child to do slow breathing exercises – start by taking a deep breath and letting it out slowly, repeating this several times. When a child is anxious and/ or having an asthma attack, say, *'Follow my finger. When it goes up, we breathe in and when it comes down again, we breathe out.'* This allows the child to focus on something other than her anxiety.

Consistency of care

In pre-school settings, it will help the child to have the practitioner (same one each time) welcome them into school, by giving them a job. This will reassure the child and distract her from her anxieties. At home, parents need to let their children get to know their babysitters before the latter look after the children in the parents' absence. Regular changes of babysitter should also be avoided.

Rewards

When children struggle to cooperate offer rewards of extra time, such as for hugs, reading a new story or playing a favourite game with them, when they comply with requests to get ready for bed, pick their toys up, let you finish a phone call, etc. Ensure you keep promises you make so that trust will grow.

Follow the child

Notice what your child is most interested in, follow his lead and build on his interests. For example, when in play a 'storm' comes, you might wonder what will happen next. State what you observe: *'That racing car is going fast!'*, *'This man is buried – oh, is he drowning? Does he need help?'* In this way the play becomes a two-way activity. The child's imagination will be stretched, and he will feel encouraged to expand his world. This in turn increases his resilience.

Repair

If the child is physically tensed up or shouting due to feeling upset by something you have done, try to repair this by apologising. It is especially important to model this repair if you caused the upset (albeit inadvertently). Notice how feeling upset is affecting the child. If in play she is throwing toys and saying things like *'this doll's going in the dustbin!'* it could be her way of showing you how upset she is. You, the adult, can make sensitive remarks on what you observe about the characters: *'That guy looks angry!'*, or *'That's a really big feeling!'*, *'Someone must have done something to upset them!'* In this way you invite the child to show you the feelings that are lying behind her actions. You can then explore the reasons and what can be done about them.

2 Trauma

Introduction

There is a prevailing assumption that infants are too young to remember traumatic events and are better served by not being involved (Eyre, Milburn and Bunston, 2020; Bunstan et al, 2016). Yet extensive neurodevelopmental research has established and widely supports the need to respond to early childhood trauma (Schore, 2006; Van der Kolk, 2015). Perry et al's (1995) pioneering research revealed that by three years of age, the child's brain is 95% of its adult size and neural pathways are profoundly affected by the child's relationships and environment. Hence relational health is pivotal to recovery from trauma even for infants (Hambrick, Brawner and Perry, 2018). Jenney (2020: 95) draws from the core attachment concepts of connection and disconnection to advocate a trauma-informed lens for strengthening family relationships when things are going well and repairing misattunement in moments of disconnection. Once traumatised children have been moved to a safe situation an important task is helping them to process early life trauma.

Calm versus alarm

Distressed children often have no words to explain their feelings since trauma creates a vacuum in expression and a fear of finding words in case what is said turns out to be true. Being overlooked is often the child's safest path. Most of us take for granted the feeling of calm or of returning to a state of calm after stress. However, this is not the case for children living with trauma and chaos. Their normal state is of high alert, which makes it impossible for them to self-regulate. This means that on becoming excited and overactive they are unable to calm down because they do not have control over their body and emotions. Schore and Sieff (2015) advises a calm environment and positive relational experiences to build new neural pathways during the first 1000 days of life. Yet Porges and Daniel (2017) warn that when children are in a state of high agitation or extreme low arousal, playfulness and creative exploration are not possible. The children need to understand their body's signals in order to relate to people. As McFie et al (2001) report, dissociation (see Glossary) for maltreated children, especially in cases of physical and sexual abuse, is a means of mentally avoiding trauma that they cannot avoid physically, and it starts in the pre-school years. Children with poor impulse control and low frustration tolerance quickly disengage in play. If sensing that they have lost the adult's attention, they may become very active, jumping and climbing over furniture. It is best then to focus on what they like to play with, invite them to name their favourite toys and try to create a script between these 'characters'.

Relational constraints

We also need to recognise and understand relational constraints that are impeding communication and the resolution of problems. Wakelyn (2020: 76) remarks that foster care training tends to focus more on physical care and behaviour management than on play, also that in busy foster homes children's fundamental needs for individual attention and intimacy are often overlooked. When children do not want to talk about what is going on for them, this is often due to their fear of the consequences they expect. We can explore the reason for this by asking them, 'What would be your worry if you were to tell someone about it?' The child can be reassured that if they tell you something you would ask their permission to tell their parent/ caregiver about it. That said, confidentiality cannot be promised when it concerns disclosures of abuse.

Joining the child

The value of engaging the traumatised child in play and of making patient observations is the insights this gives into his inner turmoil and needs. When the adult sits on the floor with the child and describes in simple words what the child is doing, the child realises that this person is giving them their full attention and is not about to go away. A comfortable, quiet environment with the TV turned off helps him to be calm and concentrate. It also helps the adult to catch the child's fleeting facial expressions and respond to cues such as when he feels ready to play or needs a rest. The child will feel safer and enjoy predictive responses. In the course of this play the adult will start to recognise likely stress factors triggering the child's fear reactions. An environment that is neither over-stimulating nor overwhelming but has just a few toys and creative materials will help her to self-regulate. You might, for example, start with a simple hand massage and a short visualisation of things the child does each day. This exercise can soften some of the harshness reflected in the punitive ways in which traumatised children may have experienced being parented. The play of a traumatised child may be very repetitive, sometimes destructive.

The child who is repeatedly crashing toy cars might be unconsciously replaying terrifying memories of unpredictable adults and changes in his life. This kind of traumatic play is likely to change gradually as he experiences the interested adult's undivided attention. Frequent periods of guided play, of 10 to 20 minutes length each, are recommended for pre-school aged children.

Children who have experienced multiple changes of caregiver worry that they are responsible for their ill fate so must be intrinsically bad. They need not just to have explanations about what happened and why (see Chapters 8, 9 and 10) but to process these upsetting events in order to realise that the abuse that happened to them was not their fault but due to circumstances that had limited their parents' ability to parent safely. They also need to realise that what happened is in the past and that they are safe now. Once children have been able to express their feelings, they will begin to realise that they will have different choices, so the past need not keep repeating itself.

Using play to address trauma

In one of the following case studies, something that helped the child to process his trauma was the use of a toy gun with foam bullets to shoot the monster plaguing his dreams. The argument is often made that play with weapons is dangerous since the child might get 'carried away'. People fear that it invites aggression – there are ethical reasons, after all, against encouraging violence. Yet many psychologists since Freud have found that children who express their feelings of aggression, fear and despair within the safety of play and in the company of a safe adult, are enabled to recognise the impact of violence and develop better self-control. In fact, Petrakopoulou's (2011: 70) study of 60 play therapists concluded that aggressive toys had no negative impact at all on children's aggressive behaviour in the play therapy process but did have cathartic value.

Key Points

- Play is a way to process traumatic events safely.
- To avoid blame and shame, it is important to clarify the reasons and background, to explain why birth parents struggled to care for children.
- Allow children to lead their play.

Case examples
Kurt, aged 4

Kurt was removed at three years of age from birth parents who were using drugs and having violent fights most days. He then suffered emotional abuse in two foster placements. When he moved to his adoptive family, Kurt was plagued by night terrors in which traumatic flashbacks took away his control of his own body, causing him to soil. Under stress, Kurt was hitting out like an infant. His school and adoptive parents were struggling to cope with all this.

HOW GUIDED PLAY THERAPY HELPED

Kurt was initially dismissive of the life story map (see case example Ivan, Chapter 10) the therapist had drawn for him to illustrate the houses he had lived in. This is a visual tool to help children who have had multiple moves explore their feelings about what has happened to them. It can be an important piece of the scenery of the child's life (Moore, 2020). He was self-reliant, having experienced grownups to be untrustworthy. Such lessons learned early in life take a long time to radically alter. As Kurt's memories resurfaced, he spoke anxiously of scary dreams. The therapist's chimpanzee puppet, Monty, told Kurt a story equating to his experience. Despite his reluctance, Kurt heard that Monty Monkey had been immensely brave and survived like him by using his wits.

Four weeks later, on seeing his life map again, Kurt chose toy figures to represent himself and the abusive foster carer, then he threw the foster carer figure into the rubbish bin. The water game (Chapter 8) helped Kurt to recognise that the 'hurting skins' (clingfilm) made it much harder to give or receive love. He became warmer towards his adoptive mum and enjoyed a story about a sad baby, whose mummy and daddy were unhappy, unable to get on or keep him safe. When the baby is taken to a safe place, he feels scared but gets looked after well by a kind family so grows up safe and loved. The story helped Kurt to feel more secure.

Each time, Kurt created stories in which 'good guys' win the battles against 'evil'. The prevailing threats in them revealed his fears of annihilation. Hearing each of his stories from the previous week reinforced the message that he was a survivor and raised his self-esteem. This replicated the 'mother-infant arousal-relaxation cycle' (see Glossary and Fahlberg, 1994; Moore, 2019) he missed in his infancy. The most influential session began with a story, *There's a Nightmare in my Cupboard* about a monster that turns out to be more scared than the child, from which Kurt took courage. As the adults discussed how to stop his nightmares, Kurt drew a monster and relished an idea that a superhero drops treacle to stop the monster in its tracks. This would give Kurt time to put the light on, shoot the monster and be rid of it once and for all. Kurt promptly led his mother and therapist to his room where toy guns with foam bullets were used to shoot the 'monster'. Twenty minutes later Kurt declared the monster gone for good. His night terrors ceased and his play began to show belief in help. He and his parents enjoyed a warm, affectionate relationship.

India, aged 3½

India, the youngest of fifteen children, was removed from parents who had drunk excessively and struggled to look after their large family. In her foster home, India showed no capacity for empathy or recognition of boundaries and was aggressive in play. She suffered frequent, prolonged tantrums and the sound of police and ambulance sirens terrified her. Though superficially affectionate, India would climb into the foster carer's lap, urinate then laugh in their face. Such rejecting behaviour was, unsurprisingly, making it especially hard for the foster carers to feel affection for her and bond with her.

HOW GUIDED PLAY THERAPY HELPED

In the second guided play session India was introduced to a life map (see explanation in previous case example, Kurt) drawn on paper. Enthusiastically she scribbled people and animals. On seeing (toy) 'birth parents' argue and (toy figures of) police and a social worker arrive, India disputed the therapist's account that the social worker had looked out for the children. Instead, she had the social worker arrested and taken to prison. India blamed the social worker for 'kidnapping' her from her birth parents. As this play progressed, India learned that when her daddy was a little boy, he was badly hurt and spent years in hospital recovering. Her birth mummy was in a wheelchair due to an accident causing such horrible pain it stopped her looking after her children. On learning that her parents had not been well cared for when they were young so did not have enough pictures in their heads to know how to look after their own children, India asked more questions about her parents' time in hospital and accepted the explanations.

Invited to experiment at dressing up, India put on a police outfit and 'locked up' her foster carer and the play therapist. She agreed to consult the wise people at 'court' on what should happen. In the role of 'judge', the therapist asked the (carer acting as) 'social worker' why she was taking the children. She said the children were scared and not being looked after properly. The 'police officer' (India) was asked what she thought should happen. India decided the parents must go to jail. In her play naughty, scary characters were jailed. The frequency of their escapes indicated ongoing fears that India was struggling to resolve. In play with puppets, she took a 'Princess' and gave the 'King' to her foster carer and whispered, *'I want you to love me!'* Taking up 'Frog', the therapist said, *'I used to be a prince and I'm waiting to be changed back'*. India decided a witch must have cast a spell on the Prince. She had Frog try to kiss the Princess, who replied that frogs were a bit slimy. India flung Frog into a corner but guarded him. As Spiderman, she 'webbed' the witch to remove her power. India went on to enjoy play with baby dolls and built a family home in clay. Within ten weeks of this intervention, she was ready to attach to her carers.

Activities
Messy Play

Playing with a variety of messy ingredients and water can be hugely beneficial in enabling children to recover missed experience of this kind of nurturing activity. Provide a large plastic mixing bowl and spoon for stirring. Help the child to mix cornflour, water and shaving foam. You might also allow the addition of other ingredients such as leftovers of cheap shampoo and

conditioner, washing up liquid, non-allergenic detergents, toothpaste, face powder, etc. Powders and spices such as paprika combined with fizzy cola can symbolise a 'volcano'. The child could add gravy granules, browning and/or cooked spaghetti. Allow the addition of small toys to the mixture to invite spontaneous storytelling. Echo feelings that emerge and share the child's thrill and delight in this play. The child could try out different mixtures on separate occasions, rather than all of them in one go.

EARLY LEARNING GOALS

ELG01: Listening and attention – this activity encourages experimentation, self-expression and recovery of nurture. Messy materials represent messy, ambivalent feelings. It also legitimises the children's right to 'make a mess'.

ELG12: Shape, space and measures – children will explore quantities, space, shapes and measures as they mix the various ingredients. They can create stories and use the information absorbed to solve problems in the rest of life.

ELG17: Being imaginative – using their imagination, children take what they have learned about materials to represent their own ideas, thoughts and feelings in original ways through the stories they create in play.

Clay families

Help the child to make clay figures of members of their birth family. Air-drying clay hardens (without baking). After drying, the models can be painted. Observe the actions taking place and conversations that develop between the figures. I recall a child building a (clay) boat to take his parents to a safe place. In such a situation you might ask the child who else he would like to have in the boat. (It might be that he chooses his caregivers who he trusts to look after him and, perhaps, his birth parents as well. Or he may wish the birth family to be taken to a place where they can no longer threaten him.)

EARLY LEARNING GOALS

ELG01: Listening and attention – this activity encourages experimentation and self-expression in ways that some children will not have experienced.

ELG12: Shape, space and measures – this activity allows children to explore the properties of dough as they make things and go on to construct stories.

ELG17: Being imaginative – children take what they have learnt about materials in original ways to represent their own ideas, thoughts and feelings through the stories they create in play.

Box as 'container'

Have a box large enough for the child to climb inside and to pull the flap over to hide herself. The child might like to line the box with fleecy fabric, or stick pictures on the walls. The box can become a safe place for playing hide and seek. You could cut out a window for the child to peep through. For some traumatised children, being ensconced in a small space, which can be lined with a fleece and cushions, gives a sense of security that is very comforting for them.

EARLY LEARNING GOALS

ELG04: Moving and handling – the child will learn to mobilise the implements he uses and move confidently, safely negotiating the space.

EG06: Self-confidence and self-awareness – this activity enables the child to be active and interactive, developing co-ordination and control in both small and large movements. It builds their self-esteem and self-awareness.

Rehearsal of daily life

With a dolls house and dolls or, say, a Sylvanian Families house and toy animals, invite the child to arrange the furniture as she pleases. Then encourage her to enact 'a day in her life'. This could begin with a visitor ringing the doorbell. Will the visitor be welcomed or someone who is not wanted? What happens next? Will the child go to school with a companion, or will there be a party? When the play comes to a natural break, talk about the feelings it arouses in each of the characters.

EARLY LEARNING GOALS

ELG01: Listening and attention – this activity encourages experimentation and self-expression in ways that the children may not have experienced.

ELG08: Making relationships – this play gives children practice at trying out roles and ways of being in relationship with others.

ELG17: Being imaginative – children take what they have learnt about materials to represent their own ideas, thoughts and feelings in original ways.

Shop play of dilemmas

In shop play, children learn ways of resolving dilemmas and making sense of other people's motivations. Taking the role of various 'customers', the parent or practitioner could act as a 'teacher' and ask the cashier how to deal with bored children who won't do as they are told. Or as 'customer', you might be a 'parent' and ask the 'cashier' (child) why your baby keeps crying and what you can do to stop it. This play can take you into explorations of the child's life experience. I have had children direct me (in the role of their 'birth parent') to steal items from the 'shop'. The child (acting as 'shop manager') calls the 'police' to arrest the thief and take her to prison. The child might then take the role of 'judge' and deliver a sentence. This kind of play leads to discussion on what a parent needs to do to put wrongs to right and keep their child safe.

EARLY LEARNING GOALS

ELG08: Making relationships – shop play gives children practice at taking turns, trying out roles and various ways of being in relationship with others.

ELG12: Shape, space and measures – in shop play, children learn about shapes, space and measures, concepts of size, weight, capacity, position, distance, time and money; they also compare quantities and objects.

ELG16: Exploring and using media and materials – this form of play enables children to learn life skills of making choices and thinking about other's needs.

Hero and transformer toys

Have a selection of hero figures and transformer toys (such as Optimus Prime), which can be altered from vehicle to human and back again. Invite the

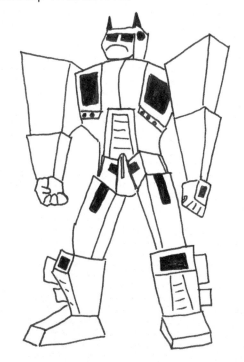

child to create stories about these characters. The stories are likely to feature battles between good and evil and, eventually, rescues – the child's means of taking on a heroic role. Afterwards you can reflect with the child on the qualities displayed by heroes, such as being helpful and kind.

EARLY LEARNING GOALS

ELG08: Making relationships – hero play gives children practice at being in relationship with others in positive ways.

ELG16: Exploring and using media and materials – this form of play enables children to learn life skills such as making choices and thinking about other people's needs.

Three wishes

Encourage the child to create a dream palace that could be set in another country or a different era. Suggest that in the garden of this dream palace, they will find exciting foods such as trees dripping in chocolate. Introduce a genie with a magic lamp. On rubbing the lamp, the child can be invited to make three wishes. What does she wish for? Think of ways her wishes can be realised, at least fictionally.

EARLY LEARNING GOALS

ELG03: Speaking – children express their ideas and learn to cooperate.

ELG06: Self-confidence and self-awareness – increases as children develop their own narratives and begin to sensitively take on others' ideas.

ELG14: The world – this activity encourages the child to recognise similarities and differences in places, objects and materials; also, to make comparisons with their immediate environment. Their observations will help them to explain why some things happen, and how things change.

Painting the monster

Traumatised children all too frequently suffer from nightmares and night terrors. Encourage the child to paint or draw a picture of the scary monster in their dream.

The child might illustrate himself being chased by the monster. Draw a speech bubble adjacent to the monster and write in it, 'Go away – leave him alone!' This will help the child to feel listened to and hopefully relieved of the bad dream.

Another way to dispose of the monster is to invite the child to shoot the picture of it with foam pellets, then tear it up and bin it. Or he might prefer to make a clay or dough model, squash it, then make something that feels worth keeping.

EARLY LEARNING GOALS

ELG01: Listening and attention – the child models on the attentive adult.

ELG05: Health and self-care – children gain mastery over their fears. This activity helps them gain control over their personal needs, including toileting.

ELG07: Managing feelings and behaviour – in time, through exploring their ideas and beliefs, children gain confidence in managing their feelings.

Dream catchers

These can be made from embroidery hoops or pieces of willow and hung above the child's bed on completion. Or they can be painted on a large sheet of paper. You might first read a story to the child about how dream catchers catch good dreams and help to make bad dreams go away. There are many such stories from North American culture that can be downloaded from the Internet.

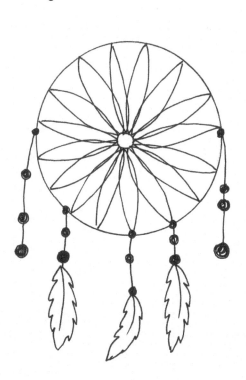

EARLY LEARNING GOALS

ELG01: Listening and attention – the child models on the attentive adult.

ELG02: Understanding – stories enable children to connect to feelings.

ELG05: Health and self-care – children gain mastery over their fears. This activity helps them gain control over their personal needs, including toileting.

ELG06: Self-confidence and self-awareness – increases as children develop their own creative ideas and begin to sensitively take on others' ideas.

ELG07: Managing feelings and behaviour – in time, through exploring their ideas and beliefs, children gain confidence in managing their feelings.

ELG16: Exploring and using media and materials – this form of play enables children to learn life skills of making choices and thinking about other people.

Scripts and strategies

Notice the emotional age

Keep in mind that children, who have been subjected to the traumas of abuse and neglect may be acting emotionally far younger (or older) than their age, especially when they are feeling especially anxious. Address the child at the age she or he is displaying. Be aware of hypervigilance (see glossary) and other symptoms of trauma. Say, 'It's a good thing you are showing me how you are feeling because I can help you to be in control of this'. Avoid letting the child see you being upset or he will sense his feelings are too much for you to handle. This will make him feel even more scared of his own power.

Rehearse testing situations

Prepare children for coping in the situations they find most stressful, such as playtime, in a noisy hall at lunchtime or assembly and school shows (when they are required to sit still). These situations whereby the child is in close proximity to others can trigger reminders of trauma quite unconsciously.

Safe space

In school or nursery provide a safe place for distressed children to go to until they feel calm enough to return to the group. Use a sand timer and when the time is up, talk to the child about ways they might alleviate their anxiety. Referral for specialist help is strongly advised for traumatised children. At home, designate an armchair as a safe space, and sit with the child.

Praise

Praise children warmly for any cooperation they show. Also praise cooperative behaviour in other children for the individual child to model on.

Reassure

When the child is struggling to cooperate, say *'Thank you, I'm so glad you are showing me how hard this is for you. We'll try again another day.'* Gently massage the child's back (over his/her clothes) – it may soothe the child.

Explanations

When children are in care due to having witnessed and been injured in the course of domestic violence, it is important to avoid blame as you explain to them why someone else (other than their birth parent) is now looking after them. Try saying something like:

> *Do you know what I think? I think your mummy was too scared to protect you when Daddy lost his temper and hurt you, which is very sad. It is your parents' job to keep you safe and I expect they wish they had. Perhaps no one made Mummy or Daddy feel safe when they were children, so they just didn't know how to keep you safe.*

The child may not understand it all but will get some idea. See Chapters 8, 9 and 10 for further ways to explain these situations and help the child to process them.

Interpret frustrations

The child who criticises the adult for doing everything wrong is likely to be projecting the despair he feels about himself on to you. Follow his wishes as much as possible. For example, say things like, *'Oh so I put this brick in the wrong place! How about you show me where it goes?'*

In play with baby dolls, a child might take the role of a caregiver who is looking after a sick baby. You could say, *'Its lovely that you want to look after this baby!'* Ask the child, *'What's the matter with the baby?'* The child may say that the baby is hungry all the time. This could be his way of telling you how much emotional care he really needs for himself.

3 Parent-child mirroring

Introduction

This chapter reflects on the quality of mirroring interactions that take place between emotionally secure parents and their infants. In this synchronous communication, mothers echo and exuberantly amplify their infant's facial, gestural and vocal expressions, which cue them to their infants' internal states (Kim and Strathearn (2014). The 'sing-song' voice they adopt is termed by Trevarthen and Aitken (1994) as 'parentese', and conveys that the baby is interesting and worthy of their parents' attention and love. Fonagy et al (2002) refer to this finely tuned responsiveness as 'reflective functioning' (see Glossary). Indeed Stern (1985) explains that the responsive mother has an instinctive ability to get inside her child's mind to understand his feelings. When her baby cries, she imitates his feelings in an empathic way, whilst signalling that she is not upset herself. Hughes (2004) refers to the 'attachment dance' to describe these vital mirroring interactions, which Porges and Daniel (2017) remind us are as visceral as they are verbal. It is how nurtured infants learn huge amounts of information on just how relationships work.

This mirroring interaction, often involving singing to the child, is very important to securing children's attachment and their healthy social and emotional development. Much of it is non-verbal, such as rocking, whispering, slow movements, facial expressions and using a gentle voice. Sadly, most abused and neglected infants miss out on this positive interaction. Too often, their parents have not experienced it in their own childhood so do not even know of its importance, let alone how to pass it on. Nevertheless, it is an experience that all caregiving parents, including foster, kinship, adoptive parents and practitioners in early years education, can replicate using the activities presented here. It is a means of helping even older children to make connections, via practicing eye contact, movements and safe touching.

The impact of stress

The 'still face' experiments of Tronick (1975), currently accessible on You Tube, demonstrate the distressing impact on infants of unresponsive mothers. Many young children who were neglected as babies will not have developed a sense of other people's needs or of safety and belonging, even after being moved to a safe family. This is because all too often the poor care their birth parents received in their own childhoods prevented them from being able to pass on healthy attachment to their children. Such a predicament will be exacerbated if the parents are too preoccupied with problems such as being unable to find any satisfying employment, being caught up in domestic violence and suffering poor mental health (Perry, 2002). Children, who are left in states of prolonged and unregulated stress have raised levels of stress hormones in their brains. Anything that causes them to feel discomfort is likely to trigger a 'fight or flight' response and result in them lashing out or running away.

When children's emotional development and social understanding has been substantially delayed, play with their caregivers is vital for enabling them to build a sense of self. Play is essential for all children to expend their energy. After all, if energy is suppressed it eventually leads to explosive bursts of frustration and anger. The mirroring relationship is crucial for enabling young children to develop a sense of security and belonging. Fun and laughter in play stimulates the 'happy' neural chemicals which help to protect the brain from the deleterious effects of anxiety and depression (Music, 2014).

How children learn

Children learn from watching their parents and caregivers' reactions. By 12 months of age, infants generally recognise their own reflection in a mirror. By 18 months, they imitate their parents in social interactions. Some show coy behaviour to hold the parents' attention. During the second year, children start using language to control their impulses. For example, saying 'Night, night!' helps the child to feel better about going to bed and being left. When parents reflect on their children's feelings, the children experience empathy and develop awareness of their internal states. An effective way to facilitate this process is for parents and early years professionals to engage children in imaginative play from which the children gain better self-control and enjoy enhanced interpersonal relationships. This is illustrated in Moore (2019, 2020), where I describe how secure attachment is enabled with older children through sharing and creating stories in play.

Key messages

- Mirror the child's expression of feeling.

- Encourage the child to express him/herself in dramatic play.

- Use sensory materials to invite exploration.

Case examples

Georgia, aged 2

Georgia resisted all methods of restraint in the form of car seatbelts, high chair, reins or her adoptive parents' attempts to hold and cuddle her. She avoided eye contact and cried for hours, unable to contain her distress. Her birth mother had been alcohol dependent and lived with a series of partners who were violent and disturbed. Georgia was left for lengthy periods, strapped into a car seat or a playpen. Her adoptive parents experienced her as a very angry child, perpetually wailing in frustration, rage and distress which they struggled to alleviate. Georgia seemed controlling, resistant and determined to be in charge, as though she was compensating for the hours she had felt completely powerless, restricted from enjoying any form of playful exploration.

HOW GEORGIA'S PARENT HELPED

Initially, mirroring play was difficult to achieve with Georgia because she would twist her body away to avoid eye contact. What proved more successful was engaging her in messy play stirring shaving foam, flour and water, or finger painting and play with play dough. Once the adoptive parents began to echo and magnify Georgia's vocalisations, modelling empathy and deep interest in her feelings, she gradually learned to trust in them. Georgia was then willing to join in mirror play and sing nursery rhymes with actions. She became calmer and made a positive attachment to her adoptive parents.

Kyle, aged 4

Kyle had been recently placed for adoption following four foster placements between frequent spells with his grandmother since the first six months of his life. His birth mother had fled to refuges to escape violent partners and she committed suicide whilst in prison for drug offences. Kyle was moved to his adoptive home shortly before his fourth birthday. Soon after this, his birth father died from drug addiction.

Kyle began to suffer disturbed sleep and his adoptive parents struggled to manage his frequent distress tantrums.

HOW GUIDED PLAY THERAPY HELPED KYLE

In play, Kyle enjoyed repeatedly rescuing the Princess (adoptive mother) from the clutches of a baddie pirate (therapist). His mother observed the therapist mirroring Kyle's expressions of feeling and learned to emulate this practice. It helped Kyle to realise the effect he was having on others and they on him. Kyle would instruct the Princess to fight the villain and then call for help. He then took the role of Peter Pan, rushed to rescue her and 'set fire' to the villain, therein enjoying a sense of victory. In the third guided play session Kyle dressed as a dragon that breathed fire to destroy the baddie. On one of these occasions, he suddenly became overwhelmed with grief and 'lay dead', reviving only when his adoptive mother gave him 'magic' plasters to heal his 'wounds'. Subsequently he had a fire engine remove the baddie. These heroic rescues are the child's means of magically contriving satisfying endings.

Kyle went on to explore scary dreams featuring his birth father. Taking the role of 'Dad', he cast the therapist as 'Kyle' and directed that she 'dream' of seeing a 'witch' who would turn out to be Dad. Then Dad turned into Superman and put out a fire. The fact that he had (fictitious) 'Kyle' rescued in his play indicated that the (real) Kyle was now feeling safer. In the next scene, Kyle as 'King' rescued a 'kind lady'. He changed into a 'kind monkey' with a 'lantern full of money' as a reward 'for being good'. Kyle further explored his sense of loss in shop play and found more ways to manage his disappointments. When a toy disappeared from the shop, Kyle compensated the customer by giving her a token to purchase *'anything she wanted'*. As he became progressively more adept at solving problems his tantrums reduced.

Activities
Mirror play
Stand (or sit) next to the child in front of a mirror and say, *'Let's copy each other!'* Point out and name your facial features. Encourage the child to copy you by pointing to and naming the same parts of their face. Make different facial expressions and encourage

the child to mirror them and show you other 'faces', which you mirror back in response.

This activity can be repeated with pointing and naming parts of the rest of the body – arms, chest, tummy, legs and toes. It will help children learn correct names for body parts while you, the adult, playfully demonstrate interest and enthusiasm for being with them.

EARLY LEARNING GOALS

ELG01: Listening and attention – in mirror play the child learns to listen, anticipate what the adult will do next, and respond with the same actions.

ELG03: Speaking – children learn to express themselves. They develop their own narratives and explanations and connect ideas.

ELG06: Self-confidence and self-awareness – when the adult mirrors and echoes the child, the child learns about consistencies. This strengthens the child's self-confidence and self-awareness to make better choices.

Attachment dance

Sit the child on your knee facing you. Tell her how warmly you feel towards her, via amplifying your own and her responses to enhance their emotional impact. This will demonstrate your deep interest and affection for the child.

> *'Wow! Look at YOU!'*
> *'Oh, isn't that AMAZING!'*
> *'It's so lovely to see your smile!'*
> *'You are so beautiful!'*

Admire the child's efforts by enthusiastically saying things like,

> *'Well done you!' 'I'm so impressed!' 'That is so lovely!'*
> *'How clever you are to* (for example) *build that model!'*

If a child has hurt herself, say,

  'Oh, poor you! That must hurt so much! You are being so brave!'

Name emotions: If a child is crying, say, *'I can see you are feeling sad.'* This helps the child who does not actually understand what he is feeling to at least give it a name. Even for crying babies, hearing the adult say with empathy, *'You are feeling sad!'* will show them that their feeling has been understood and will help them learn empathy for other's feelings.

EARLY LEARNING GOALS

ELG01: Listening and attention – children learn empathy from having it modelled to them in the exaggerated manner of 'parentese'.

ELG06: Self-confidence and self-awareness – when the adult echoes the child, the child learns about consistencies. This strengthens the child's self-confidence and self-awareness to make better choices.

Singing and movement

All around the world parents sing nursery rhymes and action songs to their children, as this is a natural way for parents to be playful with their infants.

Create a mirroring handclap routine as you sing:

  (1) Pat-a-cake, Pat-a-cake Baker's man
  Bake me a cake as fast as you can
  Pat it and prick it and mark it with 'B'
  And put in the oven for Baby and me!

For the next two songs, sit the child on your knee facing you:

  (2) This is the way the 'lady' rides, clip clop, clip clop,
  This is the way the 'lady' rides, clip, clip clop

(For other verses, replace the word '*lady*' with '*gentleman*', '*farmer*' and '*ruffian*'. At the end of the second line of the last verse, the child goes 'down into the ditch' – between the parent's knees – then is pulled back upright.)

(3) *We'll be coming round the mountain when she comes (repeat)*
We'll be coming round the mountain, coming round the mountain, coming round the mountain when she comes.

Chorus: *Singing aye yi yippee yippee yi! (repeat)*
Singing aye yi yippee, aye yi yippee, aye yi yippee yippee yi!

For the next song, sit on the floor with the child facing you. Hold the child's hands as you rock back and forth singing:

(4) *Row, row, row your boat gently down the stream*
Merrily, merrily, merrily, merrily – life is but a dream! (or)
If you see a crocodile, scream, scream, scream!

This is another hand clapping song, for which the child faces the parent:

(5) *A sailor went to sea, sea, sea,*
To see what he could see, see, see.
But all that he could see, see, see
Was the bottom of the deep blue sea, sea, sea.

EARLY LEARNING GOALS

ELG03: Speaking – children learn to express themselves. They develop their own narratives and explanations and connect ideas.

ELG06: Self-confidence and self-awareness – the nurturing attention you give children as they face you will build their self-awareness and self-confidence.

ELG16: Exploring and using media and materials – the child experiments with changing the actions and words of songs. Having fun enhances learning.

Blanket swing (needs two adults)

This activity enables children to enjoy the undivided attention and affection of two adults and can be immensely rewarding and comforting for the child. Lay a blanket on the floor and invite the child to lie in the middle of it. One of the adults stands at each end of the blanket. Both adults pick it up taking the weight of the child laid on it, then swing the blanket while singing:

> *We love you [child's name], oh yes we do!*
> *We love you [child's name], oh yes we do!*
> *And when you're far away, we're blue!*
> *Oh [child's name]we love you!*

Ensure that one parent is able to make eye contact with the child.

EARLY LEARNING GOALS

ELG01: Listening and attention – the blanket swing activity requires the child to listen to nurturing adults. From hearing them singing with warmth in their voices, the child learns to reciprocate this affection.

ELG06: Self-confidence and self-awareness – hearing his name sung by the adults strengthens the child's self-confidence and sense of security.

Sword dances (child and adult)

Sword dancing is enormous fun and helps children to learn about the space their body takes up. Use plastic or foam swords, ideally with rounded-ends.

Devise simple routines to involve you and the child in mirroring each other's movements. Have the tips of each sword meet at eye level then at waist level, and then invite the child to jump over the sword as you sweep it under their feet.

EARLY LEARNING GOALS

ELG04: Moving and handling – the child will learn to mobilise the sword and to move confidently in various ways, safely negotiating the space.

ELG06: Self-confidence and self-awareness – this activity enables the child to be active and interactive and develop co-ordination and control in both small and large movements. It also builds their self-esteem and self-awareness.

ELG08: Making relationships – this activity teaches the child how to use non-verbal signals, such as when to pretend to be injured, or 'die' and 'come back alive'. (It also encourages the idea of starting anew with a heroic identity).

Reflective sand play

Sand is ideal for sensory play as it encourages children to explore their sub-conscious thoughts and feelings.

Fill a small tray with sand and have a selection of toy figures that can be erected or buried. Invite the child to create scenery such as a beach, hills, roads and sandcastles. As you observe the actions in play use the highly animated manner of a sports commentator to comment on what is happening in the story. This is an example of narrating the play:

> *Lots of animals (or people) are fighting! Oh, the poor things are getting hurt! Ouch! What's going to happen now! I wonder if anyone can help?*

When the story characters (animals or people) get hurt, you might ask whether anyone is going to rescue them. Suggest a vet, doctor, or hospital – but don't rush too quickly to introduce help – wait and be guided by the child.

He may be trying to show you that in his experience, actually no one will help. Instead, you could say, *'I wonder how this guy is feeling? I wonder what this guy needs?'* Express admiration for the character's courage – *'Oh he's so brave!'* Show empathy for his plight. *'He must be so lonely all by himself!'*

Keeping your comments to the context of the story will allow children the privacy they need to explore their more painful feelings. Invite reflection on these feelings. Taking time to say what the child is doing will help the child value the experience of playing in the company of a deeply interested adult.

ELG01: Listening and attention – children learn to listen attentively when having this modelled to them. On hearing stories, they anticipate what will happen and respond appropriately with comments, questions or actions.

ELG07: Managing feelings and behaviour – children will talk more readily through the voice of a fictional character, about how they and others show feelings. They will discuss their own and others' actions and consequences, and will come to realise the kinds of behaviour that are unacceptable or not.

Making music to mirror feelings

This is a fun activity that is easy to provide. Most nurseries, schools will have percussion instruments. At home, if you don't have ready-made ones, try using upturned saucepans as drums and wooden spoons to bang on them. Make shakers by filling empty containers such as water bottles with pulses, lentils, etc. Use these percussion instruments to echo (mirror) sounds that convey feelings. These instruments can also be used to recreate the sounds of routines and activities (such as mealtimes and assembly). Hold a 'concert of feelings' to create sounds to represent each part of the child's day to explore how the child's day goes.

ELG16: Exploring media and using materials – singing songs and making music will encourage children to experiment at change and influencing others.

ELG17: Being imaginative – children's imagination develops in representing their ideas, thoughts and feelings through music, artistic activity and stories.

Blowing bubbles

Blowing bubbles is an excellent way to train anxious children to control their breathing, as they have to release their breath slowly in order to blow them. Bubbles can be blown through a straw into a glass or bowl, or through a wand that has been dipped in soapy water (use washing up liquid). There are increasing varieties of bubble blowers for creating larger bubbles. Children can play games of catching bubbles as well as blowing them. You might say, *'Let's see how many bubbles you pop by clapping them'*. If the hyper-aroused child gets over excited and you want to calm him you might sit him down and suggest he try popping the bubble with his finger or a toe.

EARLY LEARNING GOALS

ELG12: Shape, space and measures – blowing bubbles is a means of encouraging children to explore quantities, shapes, space, measures, recognition of which helps them to problem solve in the rest of life.

ELG16: Exploring media and using materials – the activity of blowing bubbles is relational play that will encourage children to experiment at change and influencing others.

Face painting

Painting a child's face and allowing the child to paint your face in return is a lovely activity to enhance bonding. Use non-allergenic paints and wipes. There are plenty of books available to give ideas.

EARLY LEARNING GOALS

ELG01: Listening and attention – These activities encourage experimentation and self-expression in ways that children may not have experienced. Their purpose is to enable recovery of nurture. Messy play symbolically represents messy, ambivalent feelings. It legitimises the child's right to 'make a mess'.

ELG12: Shape, space and measures: Messy play is a means of encouraging children to explore quantities, shapes, space, measures, recognition of which helps them to problem solve in the rest of life.

Making and modelling play dough

Play dough is especially comforting and pleasurable to play with while it is warm. It can be made at home (see recipe below). You can add a variety of scents such lavender and brewed camomile tea. Create stories from characters emerging from the shapes cut out.

INGREDIENTS

- 2 cups or 440g plain flour (all purpose)

- 2 tablespoons vegetable oil

- 1/2 cup or 55g salt

- 2 tablespoons cream of tartar

- Up to 1.5 cups or 355ml boiling water (adding in increments until it feels just right)

- Food colouring (optional)

- Few drops glycerine (optional – adds more shine!)

METHOD

1. Mix the flour, salt, cream of tartar and oil in a large mixing bowl.

2. Add food colouring if desired to the boiling water then stir into the dry ingredients.

3. Stir continuously until it combines into a sticky dough.

4. Add the glycerine and scents if desired.

EARLY LEARNING GOALS

ELG12: Shape, space and measures – in this activity children experiment with and explore the properties of dough as they make models and tell stories.

ELG17: Being imaginative – using their imagination, children take what they have learnt about materials in original ways to represent their own ideas, thoughts and feelings through the stories they create in play.

Scripts and strategies

Mimic 'mum and baby' interaction

With older children who have missed out on this experience, mimic the nurturing mother and baby interactions by using a gentle voice and animated facial expressions as you lie with them in a hammock or a rocking chair.

You might let the child have a drink from a nursing bottle and feed the child small pieces of biscuit or apple, while she lies on your lap looking up into your face. Let her listen to your heartbeat by putting her ear to your chest or using a stethoscope. Write messages on the child's back. Brush her hair, trying out different styles. Massage each other's hands with baby lotion.

Join in play with the child

Encourage children to express their feelings in play. Abuse can leave children believing that they are too naughty to have earned the right to be enjoying play. Remind them that while we are playing, mistakes just don't matter because play is for practicing, experimenting and trying things out.

Remember that fun and laughter releases endorphins and allow children to relax physically. You can't be relaxed and anxious simultaneously.

Invite children to try out different roles in play. In exploring these new ways of being they gain confidence and transfer skills to the rest of life.

Draw from Appendix 2, which lists more ideas for creative play.

Facial expressions

Have a chart of feeling faces and encourage the child to point to the facial expression that shows how she feels, but is unable to express in words. You can do this at the beginning and end of a play session, as usually by the end the child is more relaxed and will gain confidence from realising they feel happier.

To get a child's attention

1. Speak calmly and quietly so the child has to concentrate in order to hear you. Your calmness will soothe the child's state of agitation (Schore, 2006).

2. If the child is engrossed in play, make an effort to find out what is so interesting about the toy or game she likes best. Acknowledge her feelings about it and say when she can play with it next.

3. Then take her hands in yours and gently stroke the backs in circular motions. This entices the child to look you in the eyes and hear you better. It helps deliver your message to her brain. For children who are autistic or afraid of touch, reassure them with a light touch on their arm or a gentle back rub.

4. Now tell the child what you want her to do, for example, *'Danni, it's time to clear up'*, or *'It's time get ready for bed (or) school.'*

Mealtimes

Rather than beg the child to come and sit down at the table, offer two choices, for example: *'Do you want the red plate or the blue plate?'*; *'Would you like peas or carrots?'* The child is then more likely to come to the table to make their choice.

Avoid offering too many choices as this is likely to confuse the child who is unaccustomed to being given choices and struggles to remember the options.

Team effort

Look for ways in which you and the child can act as a team, using special signals such as high fives, linking your little finger with theirs, divising special handclaps, doing funny walks together and so on. This can help parents who are taking their child to nursery or school and getting back home again while increasing bonding. It can also help early years practitioners and special needs teachers who are seeking to build their relationship with the children they have responsibility for.

Theraplay activities

Theraplay is a play-based intervention, initiated in the USA, and established in the UK. It engages parents and children in structured play, addressing attachment with the aim of enhancing children's competence and self-regulation and enabling trust." The book *Parenting Through Theraplay* (Norris and Rodwell, 2017) describes a range of additional bonding activities. .

4 Object permanence

Introduction

During the first year of life, nurtured children absorb certain basic concepts. Following parent-child mirroring in Chapter 3, this chapter examines the next stage of child development, which occurs at around 12 months of age, when infants crawl or start to walk. They check out their surroundings and seek a reaction for signs of approval or disapproval. In this social referencing, the infant reads their parents' emotional expression to find out, *'Am I safe? Is she impressed?'* Unfortunately many vulnerable young children are restrained from this physical exploratory play. Their parents may be too anxious about the risk of injury to the child, or disapprove of him touching items such as their phones and house keys. If parents have had too little nurture or play in their own childhood, they will not have developed the neural patterns for passing on this nurturing experience to their children or even have realised the importance of enabling safe exploration of their surroundings. As a consequence, their child may exhibit a general lack of excitement or curiosity. He may try to take charge of the adult and avoid opportunities to try anything new. Lurking beneath is his anxiety at the prospect of change or surprises. To ensure his safety, the child often stays close to the parent to maintain her attention.

Exploratory play

If you show a toy to a baby of two months old, the toy may interest the baby while it is in their sight. But if the toy is removed the baby will not look for it. The object that disappears from her line of vision ceases to exist as far as she is concerned. So, let's fast-forward to four and a half months of age. Keenan and Evans (2009) cite research studies by Baillargeon (1987, 1991) in which infants of this age watched tall and short rabbits moving behind a screen and reappearing on the other side. They found the infants reached some grasp of the concept that things continue to exist even when hidden from sight much earlier than was thought possible. In fact, the more that children explore, the greater will be their comprehension of object permanence.

Let's now imagine the nurtured infant at 10 months of age checking out her surroundings. Perhaps she comes across a scarf hidden under a cushion. Infants derive immense pleasure from finding hidden objects. Her enthusiastic parent plays a game of hiding the scarf again. The child looks under the same cushion and finds it. When this process repeats enough times, she realises that this object continues to exist so even when it is hidden in new places, she knows she will eventually find it. Thomson (2020) argues that learning object permanence is one of the most significant developments for young children.

Separation anxiety

For children who have not grasped the concept of object permanence, even very temporary separations from the caregiver can raise anxiety significantly. When the parent says, *'I'll just be a minute'* and disappears for an hour, it is hardly surprising that the child's understanding of time is delayed. Being unable to predict when or if his parent will reappear heightens his anxiety. When she finally does reappear, he may cling to her fearful of her leaving him again. This makes it especially important for new caregivers such as adoptive, foster and kinship parents, when they are taking a child to pre-school, to say 'goodbye' and tell the child when they will return to take him home. It is good practice for nursery staff to support this practice rather than allow the parents to slip out of the door unseen by the child.

Through play, we can help anxious children to cope better with separation and changes in routine as well as to enjoy little surprises followed by reassurance. We can also help children to manage other anxieties affecting them, such as fear of the dark, of being left alone, fear of strangers, masks, insects, dogs, blood, the recurrence of, say, bites or wasp stings, and certain noises such as the vacuum cleaner or the toilet flushing. Hand-dryers set off accidentally can also easily frighten children who are unused to their loud sound.

Key points

- Play is practice for life and learning about protection from danger.
- Imaginary play helps children accommodate to accepting help needed.
- Sequences may repeat many times before the child moves the play on.

Case examples
Jessie, aged 4
A few months after Jessie came to her adoptive family, her delay in sensory processing was apparent. She ran into roads, crashed into furniture and tripped

over toys, heedless of warnings or hearing them too late. Jessie stepped on objects in her way as though she was in a perpetual rush. She constantly 'checked' for approval like an infant aged 12 to 18 months. Jessie's speech was difficult to follow because she was uttering only the first syllable of each word she spoke. Again, she seemed in too much of a hurry to speak clearly. When her new parents took her to school, Jessie showed high anxiety about being separated from them. Jessie's early years practitioner (ELP) tried to help Jessie make sense of why she was adopted but when she showed her photos of her birth family, Jessie, like a toddler, screwed up and threw the photos then trampled on them so the practitioner put the rest out of her reach.

HOW AN ELP HELPED JESSIE

Jessie's ELP invited in Jessie's adoptive mother and encouraged Jessie to enjoy nurturing experiences she would have missed in her large chaotic birth family. Jessie was attracted to the toy till and kept 'barcoding' the same item, as might an infant. She fed baby dolls and put them to bed then asked her mother to sing and rock her to sleep. Jessie progressed to dramatic play. To prepare her for the family's seaside holiday, a yellow cloth was spread on the floor to represent the beach. To practice crossing the road she stood at the 'kerb', pressed a 'button' and waited for the 'green light'. On reaching the 'beach' Jessie had her mother 'paddle in the sea' and 'cook a barbecue'. Next, she practiced going to the 'doctor's' and 'birthday parties' with lots of games.

Repeated rehearsal of real-life situations expanded Jessie's imagination. She began to solve problems and overcome her fears as she came to realise that certain things in life could be predicted and relied on to remain constant: in this way, she learned the principle of 'object permanence'. Playing developed Jessie's trust in her caregivers and her ability to cope better with separation.

Sam, aged 4

Recently placed for adoption, Sam tried to control everyone around him. He demanded a high level of attention and went readily to strangers, expecting them to take him with them. At school Sam had unpredictable bursts of anger and refused to share toys. He was scared that if he complied, he would never get the toy back. Sam had disturbing dreams of blood pouring from stabbings and his birth parents hiding from police. His birth parents had no example to draw from for the tasks of parenting. Their excessive alcohol consumption had led to violent squabbles. After multiple moves between relatives and foster care, Sam was experiencing adoption as a form of 'kidnap'. He was too young to understand verbal explanations and expected to be moved on soon.

HOW SAM'S ADOPTIVE PARENT HELPED

As soon as he heard admiration for his efforts, Sam would defiantly wreck the models he'd been patiently making. Inexperienced at play, he defensively ignored helpful suggestions. Instead, determined to be independent, he would refuse to let go of play dough tools when his mother offered to show him how to use them. Yet when she admired his clever thinking, Sam cooperated with storytelling and began to concede that his heroes might accept help after all.

Characters in his play started making friends. Sam began to process his life experience in a play in which a baby was kidnapped whilst fierce monsters distracted the mother. His new parent wondered what would happen to this baby. Sam had the 'mother' take 'baby' to the 'park', where she thought he'd be safe. But a 'ghost' (symbol of the past) snatched the baby. The mother said how confusing it was, and asked who could help. Sam had the 'baby' rescued and the 'ghost' jailed, now accepting that children need to feel safe.

Activities
Peek-a-boo
These games give practice at separation.

Young children love to play peek-a-boo, a game which allows them to feel a frisson of fear as something pops into view.

To play this game, cover your eyes with your hands, then uncover them and playfully say, *'Boo!'* The child has a turn and the game can keep repeating until the child tires of it. You can also hide behind a door and peek out, saying, *'Here I am!'*

EARLY LEARNING GOALS

ELG01: Listening and attention – in games of 'peek-a-boo', the parent, caregiver or practitioner teaches the child how to listen and respond appropriately by role-modelling how to do this. It is a safe context for the child to practice coping with separation from parents or carers for short periods.

Hide and seek

Games of hide and seek can be huge fun. It can start with taking turns at hiding objects in a tray of sand for the other person to find. Or the child may hide toys or him/herself, say, behind a curtain or piece of furniture. The adult closes her eyes and counts aloud to 20, then says, *'Ready or not here I come!'* Look in places such as under the table or behind the door and in an animated tone, wonder, *'Where can she be? I can't see her anywhere!'* Laugh and rejoice when you find her, calling out to her, *'Oh there you are!'*

As the game keeps repeating, children realise that they or their toy will be found even when out of sight. They also learn to deal with intense emotions of anxiety *'Will she find me?'* and those of thrill and excitement when, on being found, they seek a more secret hiding place.

EARLY LEARNING GOALS

ELG01: Listening and attention – in games of hide and seek the parent or caregiver teaches the child how to listen and respond appropriately by role-modelling how to do this. It is a safe context for the child to practice coping with separation from parents or carers for short periods.

ELG16: Exploring and using media and materials – exploring their territory will increase the child's understanding and ability for problem solving.

Puppet play

Provide a selection of glove puppets, which can easily be made from socks with buttons sewn on for eyes, or use finger puppets or dolls. Each participant introduces a character, names him or her, and states what the character likes doing and something they're scared of.

(1) Encourage the child to dramatise the characters helping each other out. For instance, a bigger animal could help a nervous hedgehog to cross a 'wobbly bridge' or 'busy road' to reach safety.

As the child joins in she learns to anticipate and prepare for possible danger via planning ways to avert dangerous risks and practice for real life situations.

(2) Involve the child in a game of hide and seek that develops into a story. Perhaps a prince or princess gets lost and is eventually found. Have a party and games to celebrate the character being found. Let the child answer the following questions and suggest answers only if the child is really stuck:

Suggested Questions

Did the princess/prince want to hide (or) get lost?

Did the princess/prince want to be found?

Did the others know where to look?

How did the princess/prince feel while she was waiting – excited or upset?

How did it feel for her/him to be found – Pleased? Disappointed? Excited?

EARLY LEARNING GOALS

ELG08: Making relationships – children take account of others' ideas and show sensitivity to others' needs and feelings.

ELG17: Being imaginative – these activities enable children to develop ideas about how to imaginatively represent their own thoughts, ideas and feelings.

Pictorial clocks

While digital clocks are more commonly used, illustrated analogue clocks are more useful for teaching children about time. Create a daytime clock (7am to 7pm) with the child. For each hour, illustrate a related activity such as waking up, getting dressed, eating breakfast, going to nursery or school, having elevenses, doing an activity, having lunch, going home, eating tea, playing, and bedtime rituals. See Appendix 3 for a sample template.

ELG12: Shape, space and measures – pictorial clocks are especially useful as visual reminders to help children anticipate what is going to happen and when it will happen. In this way you enable them to recognise patterns and realise what can be safely predicted. This helps insecure children to feel more confident and in control of what is happening to them in the rest of their life.

Photo boards

Take photographs of staff, objects and areas in the building and arrange them on a board at a height the children see. This makes the place easier for children to relate to as it is who and what they actually see.

ELG12: Shape, space and measures – photo boards are especially useful as visual reminders to help children anticipate what is going to happen and when. In this way you enable them to recognise people and patterns and realise what can be safely predicted. This helps insecure children to feel more confident and in control of what is happening to them in the rest of their life.

Calendars

Pictorial calendars can be made to illustrate regular routines, also planned moves to show the child how many days (or sleeps) until the next move, what to expect on that day, and who will be involved in each event/activity. For planning a child's move see Appendix 9.

Developing Secure Attachment

ELG12: Shape, space and
measures – pictorial calendars
are especially useful as visual
reminders to help children
anticipate what is going to
happen and when. In this way
you enable them to recognise
patterns and realise what can be
safely predicted. This helps insecure children to feel more confident and in control
of what is happening to them in the rest of their life.

SUN.	MON.	TUES.	WED.	THURS.	FRI.	SAT.

ELG16: Exploring and using media and materials – exploring their territory will
increase the child's understanding and ability for problem solving.

Clay modelling

Encourage and help the child
to make clay models of people
(and/or animals). These models
can then be used to represent
various characters in a story.
This allows the child to explore
any confused feelings he has
within the privacy of the story
being about someone else. Have
these figures talk to each other.
Follow the child's lead and
notice their expectations of how
people treat each other.

If the child expresses anger towards a 'parent' figure, it is important to show empathy
for his feelings: The EYP/caregiver could say, *That's a really upsetting feeling!'* This
helps to avert the risk of the child feeling ashamed of having wrong feelings. Be
aware that his anger towards the current caregiver is probably being carried over
from previous times when he felt let down. The child may want to bash a (clay) figure
representing the parent experienced as abusive. The EYP/caregiver can reassure the
child by saying things like, *'You are safe now'.* Demonstrate genuine interest in his
thoughts, ideas and views.

ELG01: Listening and attention – in this activity the child learns how to listen and respond appropriately from the adults role-modelling how to do this.

ELG12: Shape, space and measures – this activity enables children to learn properties and characteristics of clay, such as its changing form as it dries. The child realises that change is possible.

ELG16: Exploring and using media and materials – using tools and techniques, and experimenting with texture, form and function will increase the child's understanding and ability for problem solving.

Heuristic play

The term 'heuristic play' was defined by child psychologist Elinor Goldschmeid in the 1980s. It is used to describe children's play with, and exploring of, the properties of objects from the real world. It might involve play with items such as dishcloths in a bowl of water, or with clothes pegs. It could involve banging spoons on an upturned saucepan, or playing with natural objects, such as

leaves, acorns, twigs, making daisy chains – the possibilities are endless.

The point of this play is to ignite children's curiosity and to replicate the thrill of discovering simple pleasures that nurtured babies and toddlers enjoy, but many less fortunate children are likely to have missed out on.

ELG12: Shape, space and measures – as children explore and experiment with the properties of these objects, how the objects look, smell, taste, feel and sound, they recover the play experience that most children experience at an earlier age.

ELG16: Exploring and using media and materials – exploring their territory will increase children's understanding and ability for problem solving.

ELG17: Being imaginative – children use what they have learnt about materials in original ways, thinking about their uses and purposes. They represent their own ideas, thoughts and feelings through imaginative, creative and dramatic play and story making.

Hidden object books

Encourage children to find objects that are hidden in a picture. This will help them to concretise the concept that objects exist independently, even when they are hidden from view.

The publisher Usborne sells a variety of these kinds of books, many of which are aimed at younger children. Pop-up books are also effective for providing surprises, sometimes hidden under a flap.

EARLY LEARNING GOALS

ELG01: Listening and attention – in this activity the child learns how to listen and respond appropriately from the adults role-modelling how to do this.

ELG12: Shape, space and measures – finding hidden objects will help children to recognise and describe patterns and objects.

ELG17: Being imaginative – reading stories will stretch children's imagination and stories that are solution focussed will develop their ideas about how to resolve their own feelings and problems.

Scripts and strategies
What is causing the child's anxiety?

The child may be worried about something at school or home. By joining the child in her play with, say, a dolls house and dolls, you encourage her to share her worries. Ask her to let the dolls (the child names) show you what has been happening and what the people (in her narrative) do next. Encourage the child to share memories and thoughts in play that frees her to reveal her fears and process them safely. Make careful notes of what you hear and observe.

Acknowledge and label the child's feelings: *I can see you're really upset!*

Listen attentively

Your calmness will calm the agitated child. Encourage the child to tell you the whole story of his worries. Ensure that you allow enough time for this.

Use 'TED' questions: Tell – Explain – Describe.

Scaling the fear

Frightened children may have to be persuaded gradually to engage in pretend play. Let's imagine the child, who struggles to articulate words, is picking up a truck. As the adult, you might respond by putting a car on the 'road' and say, *'Drive carefully! We don't want an accident.'* The child will copy you and gradually learn to express himself. Invite him to rate how scared he is feeling by pointing to the relevant part of his body and asking; *'Is it just a little bit, like up to your ankles, or a bit more – up to your knees, or worse – up to your tummy, or worse still – up to your shoulders or head (meaning very scared)'*. This will also help the child to develop a sense of perspective and be less scared of feeling ashamed of his fear, frustration and inadequacy.

Routine

Prediction is highly important to anxious children. After all, so much of life is outside their control. For this reason, regular routines help them to feel more confident about knowing what to expect and when things will happen.

Remind of past success

Show children how very important their feelings are to you. Remind them that they have managed to cope well before and can do so again. You might say something like, *'Remember last Friday you helped me make that lovely cake? I know how brave and clever you are – so will you help me out again?'*

Respect the child's wishes

Children will often use play to convey their anxieties about separation. When their play features themes of war and devastation it could be their way of showing you how they are feeling about being left. You might ask, *'What will happen when the soldiers shoot these people? How will they feel?'*

Alternatively, the child might respond in the opposite way and turn his back on you as though to say, *'I'm not interested. I don't need you!'* You might respond gently, *'I am happy to pass you more pieces when you want them'*. This may encourage his engagement and increase his trust very gradually.

Don't let your own anxiety get in the way

Sometimes parents and caregivers who feel anxious about separation and the prospect of rejection can miss the child's cues. In the scene above, they might ask the child to make the soldiers happy so there will be no need for a war. Let's suppose the child is playing out a scene in which baby pigs are being separated from their mummy pig. Rather than discuss what is going on, the anxious caregiver might announce *'it's time for tea'*. In so doing she loses the opportunity to explore how the piglets (and her child) are feeling about what is happening. If the child is using play to explore his experience of painful separation, he might have Piglet say, *'I don't like you!'* The anxious adult might feel offended and say, *'Well, then I don't like you either!'* In giving this response, she misses the chance to find out why Piglet said what he did and what can be done to help him feel better about things.

Practise separation

At home, rehearse situations such as going to school and crossing roads, arriving at school, hanging up their coat, finding a teaching assistant who can give the child a task, then the child saying goodbye to mum. This can be acted out in person or by using toy figures to represent the people.

In pre-school settings, have pictures of a puppet hanging its coat up and playing in each area of the setting. These pictures or photos can be made into a leaflet for the child to take home and look through prior to and when she or he starts pre-school. In the educational setting, practitioners can reassure the anxious child by showing him photos of the parent who is collecting him.

Transitional object

The energy of anxious children dips at certain periods in the school day, often when it's noisy, such as in the school playground or hall at lunchtime or in a corridor. To counter this anxiety, the early years practitioner could ask the caregiver to provide the child with a small item, such as a piece of fabric that has their scent on it. The child can keep it in his pocket to remind him of his parent when he needs reassurance – this is described as a transitional object (see Glossary). Parents or caregivers could leave an item of theirs for the child to look after until they return to collect him. It might be an old T-shirt the parent has slept in and therefore has their scent on it. The child can keep the item in his bag. Some children find this easier to understand, expecting the parent to return for this item (if not just for them).

5 Cause and effect

Introduction

To be able to recognise the effect we have on others and they have on us is essential to being in satisfactory relationships. In the first year of life nurtured children learn that they can cause things to happen, which will have an effect on their parent (see Glossary for cause and effect). For example, when the child drops something such as a toy, the patient parent picks it up and gives it back to the child. This is a process that repeats many times and conveys to the child that his action has an effect so he must be worthy of attention. Keenan and Evans (2009: 241) refer to research which shows that the amount of time a mother engages with her baby will affect her child's success at recognising emotions in other people.

Children who are not regularly attended to are slower to learn about the consequences they and their actions have on others. Some parents are intermittently responsive to their child and when parental attention is too unpredictable the child can never be sure of a response. As a result, he either gives up or clings to the parent to keep her in his sight. The child who receives only random responses learns that curiosity doesn't pay and ceases to show it. Young children are highly dependent on parents to regulate their emotional states by comforting them when they show distress and calming them down when they are over aroused. The abused child who has not experienced consistent comfort will not have learned how to manage his feelings so is more likely to react to situations in a highly-strung manner.

Consequences of unpredictable care

Many vulnerable children become adept at disguising their inadequacies. The previous chapter reflected on anxieties that arise from having missed out on learning the principle of object permanence. This chapter explains the resulting behaviour that wears out the responsiveness of caregivers and risks perpetuating legacies of rejection. An example is the child, who repeatedly demands that the caregiver look at him, praise him or pay him complements. Desperate to feel he is worthy of attention, the child will keep making demands because he is not able to gain the reassurance he craves via the reward of completing tasks. To avert the risks of criticism, disapproval and rejection, the child may nod his head as if he has understood things he actually has not. This is because he is trying to avoid shame and disapproval, which in his experience threatens further rejection. This makes it difficult to discover just how little he really knows. High levels of anxiety can also leave the child unwilling to engage in play activities with which he is unfamiliar.

Some babies and young children get passed round lots of babysitters who are not always safe. As a result, the child will not have learned to differentiate between strangers and parents. The child who is oblivious to danger may smile coyly at strangers and seek attention and affection indiscriminately in the hope of getting some sort of reward in response. He figures, *'If I'm nice to her, she might give me some sweets!'* Caregivers often worry about such a child who will 'go to anyone'. The affection he shows them seems enchanting at first but soon comes to feel superficial. This is unrewarding and makes it harder for these parents and early years professionals to bond with him. Consequently, the child's sense of self-worth takes a further dive.

The importance of play

Play is recognised for its value in providing practice for life. In play, failure does not matter because experimenting is essential to find out what works. This is an important message to convey to children whose past lack of success has discouraged them from risking a repeat of humiliating failure.

Wakelyn (2020: 77) advises that, 'Child-led play with the full attention of the primary caregiver for short periods of time is central to interventions with young children with psychological vulnerability or developmental delay'.

Dramatic play involving caregivers is especially valuable for helping children to learn about the impact they have on others. This can be contrived in a way that will build security in their attachment relationships. It can involve dressing up, puppets and 'small world' toy figures, and allow children to reenact their experience and create new outcomes that will help them reconcile to their situation. It will also help build their resilience for coping with disappointment.

Key points

- The safety of play enables a scared child to tolerate physical proximity.
- Having an adult reflect on things said enables feelings to be processed.
- Kidnap is a common theme in play of children in care and adopted.

Case examples

Conor, aged 4

Conor presented as a 'frozen' unattached child. His foster mother worried that he would 'go off with anyone'. His birth mother had been abused, raised in care and depended on drugs. Conor had been left with a variety of sitters but was found on his own when he had to be rescued from a house fire. His foster carer experienced him as demanding yet frightened when she came near him. His destructiveness put her off trying to engage him in play. Conor crashed his toy cars repeatedly. His power rangers and animal toys violently knocked out their competitors and 'killed' each other with ferocity. The action in play suggested that Conor had witnessed a lot of violence. He disregarded any suggestion of rescue and his stories invariably ended with the demise of the injured. Conor would insist, *'No one could mend them!'* His belief that everything ended in annihilation reflected his real-life experience.

HOW GUIDED PLAY THERAPY HELPED CONOR

Taking the role of Peter Pan, the play therapist invited the 'dog' (a string puppet that Conor was manipulating) to make friends. Conor accepted the invitation. The therapist remarked that when she asked in this friendly way, he was friendly back. But then, dressed as a dinosaur, Conor proceeded to threaten Peter Pan. The therapist wondered if the dinosaur needed a friend. Conor nodded and took up 'PC Plod' who invited these friends back to his house for *'tea and cakes'*. His foster carer joined in this play. Although Conor had been very frightened of physical proximity to adults, the safety of the play situation allowed him to tolerate it with the adults present since it was just 'pretend'. As Conor began to relax and feel less scared his play became less violent and frenetic. He learned to trust his foster carer sufficiently that by the time he moved to his adoptive family he was be able to make a more secure attachment to them and soon settled.

Jasmine, aged 4

Jasmine, aged 4, was parted from her brothers when she and her siblings were removed from learning-disabled parents who suffered poor mental health. Jasmine had several changes of care within her extended family but very little nurturing attention. After a year in foster care she was placed in an adoptive family. Jasmine began tearing out her hair and wrecking her toys. Her adoptive parents were shocked but did not realise how frightened she was. Sadly, they felt too embarrassed at their lack of competence to ask for help. Three months later, Jasmine was returned to her (previous) foster placement, believing she was to blame for the adoption breakdown. These foster carers became weary of her dependence on set routines of repetitive hand washing. A very frightened child, perpetually on the alert to anticipated rejection, she was merely trying to control everything she could. Jasmine was fortunately moved to another foster family, who were therapeutically trained.

HOW GUIDED PLAY THERAPY HELPED JASMINE

Jasmine was instantly drawn to dressing up. In play she orchestrated being 'kidnapped'. She directed her foster mother to be 'Father Christmas' and the therapist to be a 'witch' who was to threaten to steal the 'two-year-old child' (Jasmine). Sitting on Father Christmas's lap, Jasmine asked for a magic wand. In response to the therapist's suggestion that the wand could allow children to choose which age they wished to be, Jasmine promptly had the therapist leave the room and re-enter as the 'nasty witch' who abducts her. The therapist complied, saying, *'Where is the girl? I'm going to take her away!'* The foster carer in role as Father Christmas asserted very firmly that she wouldn't allow this to happen, therein conveying to Jasmine that she was safe and would be looked after properly. But Jasmine directed the witch to steal the girl's wand, not quite ready to trust in her improving fortune. Even so, in the next scene Jasmine decided the 'child' was now older and strong enough to retrieve the wand. As a means of keeping safe, she had the 'witch' change into a 'kind, friendly person'. Many variations of this story were repeated over several weeks. Jasmine had the foster mother act as a 'kind mum, who falls asleep', while directing the therapist to steal the 'child' and say, *'I'm your real mum! Come with me!'* The 'caring mum' (foster carer) woke and searched for the child, stating how much she loved her and wanted her to be safe. Jasmine directed that the 'next night' the 'kind mother' be captured. The 'child' searches for her mother and eventually finds her in 'prison'. Jasmine directed the therapist as 'kidnapper' to state, *'If I can't have you, I'm not going to let you have your new mum!'* Hearing the 'kind mother' express her despair, Jasmine was prompted to have the kidnapper 'fall asleep' (enabling 'the child' to be rescued) and told her, *'Now you know how it feels to be locked up!'* The play ended with her transformation into a 'kind granny'.

Jasmine's reflection that, *'This was like having two mums being nice to you!'* revealed her appreciation of having the undivided attention of two interested adults. In another play a *girl* and her *best friend* were kidnapped repeatedly and 'injured'. Jasmine decided hugs and cuddles would heal their injuries.

Her fears of kidnap were understandable given the number of changes of care she had experienced as rejections and proof that she was unlovable. As she worked though her paralysing anxiety, what brought about the profound change was having the adults follow her directions and show sensitivity to her feelings. This enabled Jasmine to reconstruct her self-image as someone worthy of attention. She could now exercise her power in far healthier ways.

Activities
Balloons and balls

Physical activities can provide huge amounts of fun and are a way of releasing endorphins that stimulate happy chemicals in the brain.

Play games of keeping balloons in the air, using hands and feet. Have soft lightweight balls, of varying size and texture (sponge or plastic) to throw and catch, play football, roll the ball to each other or roll them at skittles.

EARLY LEARNING GOALS

ELG04: Moving and handling – these games develop co-ordination, control, and movement in the child's interaction with others. Children gain confidence from moving in a range of ways and safely negotiating their space.

Swordplay story

Swordplay is valuable for learning about the space one's body takes up. The child also learns how to intercept and use social signals. Before starting swordplay, try the activity "Sword dances (child and adult)" in Chapter 3 as a warm up exercise to convey social signals and establish safety rules.. You can then invite the child to join you wearing pirate hats and creating a story. The story might begin with a fight over territory, or pirates landing on a desert island, and having to survive threats such as sharks and intruders.

Developing Secure Attachment

ELG04: Moving and handling – these games develop co-ordination, control and movement in the child's interaction with others. Swordplay facilitates learning about space, taking account of others' ideas and showing sensitivity, which in turn enables children to have more positive relationships.

ELG06: Self-confidence and self-awareness – having fun encourages children to try new activities and to say why they like some things more than others.

ELG08: Making relationships – forming positive relationships builds confidence and a sense of self-worth. Children learn from the adults' reactions how to play cooperatively, follow rules, take turns, incorporate others' ideas, reach agreement and show sensitivity to needs and feelings.

Obstacle course

This activity can be carried out indoors or outdoors in a back yard or garden. It will encourage the children to socialise and cooperate in completing tasks.

BUILD AN OBSTACLE COURSE

- Pull string through upturned plant pots, to use as the handles of stilts to walk on.

- Using boxes and chairs make tunnels to crawl through, step on, climb over and squeeze under.

- Spread out cloths for crawling under.

- Erect sticks upright in the ground for the child to weave between.

- Lay a ladder on the ground to hopscotch over.

EARLY LEARNING GOALS

ELG04: Moving and handling – this activity will improve the children's physical dexterity while they have fun and develop their control and co-ordination.

ELG06: Self-confidence and self-awareness – this activity builds the child's confidence as they learn to move in a range of ways, negotiate the use of the space and gain more self-awareness, all of which encourages a sense of competence for trying out new activities and socialising with other children.

Construction and sequencing

Constructing models is an important part of learning as it involves sorting and arranging parts in sequences as well as building. It enables the adult to demonstrate to the child how to cope with failure and not feel destroyed or discouraged when things don't go to plan. Teach simple sequences:

(a) build towers of bricks;

(b) erect dominoes and let them fall over;

(c) build sandcastles – fill a cup with sand, tip it over, tap its base then lift the cup;

(d) collage – requires glue to be applied to paper *before* the glitter;

(e) simple construction kits (Duplo is easier than Lego for under-fives).

Encourage the child to build houses, carriageways and other forms of scenery. By doing so, she practices patience and dexterity.

EARLY LEARNING GOALS

ELG07: Managing feelings and behaviour – children learn to cope better with disappointments. From creating sequences and observing consequences (see Chapter 3) children will talk about feelings and outcomes.

ELG12: Shape, space and measures – children learn about the relative size, weight, capacity, position and distance of objects. They also compare features, quantities and solve problems.

Dramatic play – fairy stories

Children create their own stories in dramatic play. To ignite their curiosity and inspire imagination provide a variety of props, such as bags, purses, hats, wigs, shoes, play money, clothes and pieces of cloth. Clothing can be created from blankets or sheets that can be also act as 'scenery' spread over floor or chairs, or make a den or a castle, for example.

A scene could begin with a king trying to assert his authority over a servant. Let's imagine the servant gets upset at being bossed around. Explore feelings that arise in the course of play and demonstrate ways to use authority wisely.

You might like to start by reading a traditional fairy story such as *Cinderella*, *Hansel and Gretel*, *The Snow Queen*, *Jack and the Beanstalk* or *Goldilocks and the Three Bears*.

These stories illustrate predicaments with which many young children are familiar, such as sibling rivalry, parental favouritism, scapegoating, conflict, and also neglect. The way in which children lead their play often reveals their preoccupations and the direction they want it to go. New ways forward can then be proposed. For example, after reading *Jack and the Beanstalk* you could invite the child to dress up as Jack. Ask if he can find a friend to help him deal with the giant. Or, on reading *Cinderella*, ask who would like to be fairy godmother and how might she help the child?

EARLY LEARNING GOALS

ELG07: Managing feelings and behaviour – dramatic play enables the child to talk about their feelings and find out how to show feelings. In the safety of the fictional context, children take notice of people's behaviour, how their own affects that of others in turn, and come to realise which behaviour is unacceptable.

ELG08: Making relationships – the child gains an understanding of the need for rules, and learns to cooperate and adjust to different situations.

ELG17: Being imaginative – this form of play stimulates imagination. Children begin to think from others' perspectives, and adapt new insights to real life.

Dominoes

Dominoes easily fall over when touched, hence are ideal to demonstrate 'cause and effect' consequences, and ways to handle frustration.

Tell a short story that illustrates what happens when things go wrong. It could be about a child who as a result of going to bed late gets up late, and then is late getting to school, which leads to more problems. Involve the child in erecting a domino to represent each decision the child makes, albeit by default. As something happens (like the child falling into a puddle), push the first domino and watch the row fall. Talk about how one thing affects another, which then affects another and so on.

DOMINO GAMES

Using a dice, throw a six to start. Each person has a turn picking up a domino from the pile and placing it to match the correct number of the domino either end of the row. Dominoes can also be used for construction – see the Construction and sequencing activity.

EARLY LEARNING GOALS

ELG08: Making relationships – by involving the child in playing out the story about consequences followed by games with dominoes, children learn to recognize the reasons for rules, cooperation, taking turns and showing sensitivity to others' needs and feelings.

ELG17: Being imaginative – learning about consequences in a variety of ways can expand children's imagination.

Masks

Masks can be useful for exploring feelings. The child can draw a cross face on one and a happy face on another. While holding the cross mask over their face they can be encouraged to say what makes them feel

cross, and while holding the happy face mask, they could say what and who makes them happy.

Another way to use masks is to depict the character as a hero or villain. By wearing the hero mask, the child assumes the authority and persona of the character. The mask lends safety and privacy to show feelings in the fictional play context which the child may sense are not really allowed in real life.

Use torn strips of paper to make papier mâché masks.

1. Soak the strips of paper (newspaper or kitchen roll are the most absorbent) in a mix of PVA glue and water. Apply in layers over a mould such as a blown-up balloon. Use an extra lump of paper to mould a nose on both sides of the balloon.

2. When the balloon has dried, cut it vertically into two halves so they can be used to make two masks..

3. Cut out holes for eyes etc. and punch small holes in each side, through which to fasten string to attach the mask to the head.

4. Paint the mask.

EARLY LEARNING GOALS

ELG04: Moving and handling – this activity will improve children's physical dexterity as they use a range of materials.

ELG16: Exploring and using media and materials – Mask-making will enable the child to learn about processes of physical change, from seeing the balloon dried out, cut and transformed into a mask.

ELG17: Being imaginative invites imaginative dramatic play and the development of skills in negotiating around others' ideas.

Models

Papier mâché (using the glue-soaked strips of paper) can similarly be used to make objects such as bowls to keep things in, or to make models of, say, people and animals, which can be painted when dried and used in dramatic play.

ELG04: Moving and handling – this activity will improve children's physical dexterity as they use a range of materials.

ELG16: Exploring and using media and materials – model-making will enable the child to learn about processes of physical change, from seeing the models that they have seen transformed from a wet substance serving a new purpose once they have dried out.

ELG17: Being imaginative invites imaginative dramatic play and the development of skills in negotiating around others' ideas.

Scripts and strategies
Addressing difficult feelings

ANGER

First, acknowledge the child's feelings. Say, '*I can see you're feeling very cross/annoyed about this rule!*' Then explain: '*But here the rule is no sweets before meals*' or '*the rule is no hitting*' or '*no running off*' etc. The child is likely to protest. Stay calm and clarify: '*It's because we care about you and want you to be safe, healthy, and to have fun and friends to play with.*'

In the play situation, notice when angry feelings are being expressed through the child's fictional characters. Respond by saying something like this: '*Elephant sounds very cross* [or sad, upset]*! – I wonder if anyone can help?*'

Even if the child shows no reaction, ask, '*Does Elephant need a friend?*'

Try not to let the child feel ashamed of his undesired feelings. Instead, encourage him to express his anger by, for example, thumping or throwing a pillow, bashing a lump of clay, ripping (unwanted) paper, singing loudly, banging a drum, kicking a ball against a wall, or stamping his feet.

CONTROL

When your child wants to be boss, acknowledge her desire. '*Oh, so you want to be in charge!*' In play, introduce another 'character' and say, '*Teddy wants to be the boss too!*' Have a playful discussion about who should be in charge and why, but avoid becoming competitive with the child. Notice her need or wish and respond in a way that acknowledges her feeling but keeps the safe boundary. For instance, say humorously,

'You might think that's ok, but Mum [or you as carer/ELP] *is in charge around here! It's my job to keep you safe'.*

Give clear instructions but avoid arguing with the child. Instead say, *'Who's going to be first to the bathroom? – Ready-steady-go!'*

AGGRESSION IN PLAY

There are several reasons why children are destructive while playing. They might be operating at an emotionally younger age and not understand why force is unnecessary (for example, to take things apart and find out how they 'work'). Lack of sensory integration means that the child might be unaware of how much strength they are using (see Chapter 6). Others show aggression in the manner shown them by (birth) parents who might have dealt with conflict in this way. The children need help to learn a more satisfactory way of relating.

If the child is aggressively tugging at your hair, suggest she pulls a doll's hair. Invite the behaviour you prefer to see: say, *'Hugging feels nice!'* In a battle the child is carrying out between (toy) people you might say, *'Don't these guys need a doctor?'* If the 'doctor' gets angry, admit, *'Yes even doctors get angry; maybe someone hit the doctor.'* In this way you validate negative feelings, and help the child realise that there must be a genuine reason for these feelings. The more nurturing attention we give children the sooner their anger will reduce and their fears (behind the anger) diminish.

Managing challenging behaviour

LIMIT SETTING

Every time you set limits on behaviour try to increase the time you spend playing with the child – it will help you find out what is preoccupying him. Play gives children ways to express their concerns in less provocative ways. Avoid using the sanction of restricting his playtime with other children since this will be detrimental to your child's development. Giving children 'time out' away from others is a common strategy as it allows them to calm down when things go awry. Often the child is sent to their bedroom. This is not always effective since some children actually prefer to be isolated. When children do need time out, try the activities listed under the 'time out' activities heading. Limit time spent on playing online games and TV and have earlier bed times. Give the child helping tasks.

Use sand timers to:

(1) Limit screen time.

(2) Encourage turn taking – the timer ending means it's someone else's turn.

(3) Let the child know the activity is coming to an end. When the timer buzzes it is time to stop play and tidy up. This reduces the shock and upset at the unexpected sudden ending.

(4) Use the timer for 'calm time'.

TAKES WITHOUT ASKING

If the child takes someone else's property, first acknowledge how badly he wanted this item and say, '*Tell me when you need another (snack/new pencil etc.) and I'll see how soon we can find you one*'. Talk to the other adults involved in the child's care about providing healthy snacks for breaks.

AVOID CONFUSION

Show the child what is needed: for example, when it's time to go, pick him up or put a supportive hand at his back, rather than telling him what to do. Simplify your instructions by saying: '*Let's do this*' instead of '*Could you tidy the toys away / put your coat on?*' etc. Make it easy by doing things with him, so he can't fail at the task. Use rewards but avoid bribes, sanctions and penalties.

ENABLE CALM

Calming bottles provide something for the child to focus on and to calm down. They can be purchased online but are also easy to make. To make your own version, fill a bottle with warm water, glitter glue and food colouring. Add glitter, shake, and the ingredients will make swirly patterns.

'Time out' activities

Turning a negative into a positive: Scrunch sheets of newspaper into balls and invite the child to throw them (hoopla style) into a wastepaper bin. Sit with the child and join in throwing them. Then encourage the child to tear the paper into strips. The strips can be used subsequently for papier mâché projects such as the masks and models above. This helps to turn the negative emotion into a positive sense of achievement.

Use up surplus energy: Encourage the child to use surplus energy in physical exercise such as the trampoline, or sensory play with sand (see Chapter 6).

BEDTIME SOOTHING

Play soothing music at bedtime. Avoid getting into arguments at bedtime. Say, *'Tomorrow is another day and we'll try again, so don't worry!'*

CONFLICT RESOLUTION

HighScope Conflict Resolution is an established tool designed for children in early years and primary school settings to enable them to solve problems by learning the steps required to recognise, discuss and resolve conflicts. Ellen Booth Church's (2021) article refers to this conflict resolution approach designed by Betsy Evans of the High/Scope Educational Research Foundation. Her six steps are as follows:

1. Approach children calmly, stopping any hurtful actions.

2. Acknowledge children's feelings.

3. Gather information about what happened.

4. Restate the problem and reflect back what you understand about it.

5. Ask for ideas for solutions and choose one together.

6. Be prepared to give follow-up support. Give lots of positive praise!

6 Physical development

Introduction

Fresh air, physical exercise and an adequate diet are essential to children's healthy development. Young children need to be able to run around, jump and play, climb up and down stairs and so on. Not to be able to do so is bound to have a negative effect on their emotional wellbeing as well as their physical development. Sadly, records reveal that prior to removal from a neglectful situation, some infants are left for lengthy periods strapped into car seats, buggies, or playpens (Howe, 2005). This restriction of their movement impedes their ability to explore and use their bodies fully. Development of physical strength and agility is further diminished when these children have inadequate food and exercise. I recall a foster carer remarking that he noticed the lack of core body strength in the fostered children he lifted compared with his more nurtured grandchildren. Furthermore, there are disproportionately large numbers of children in foster care found to be suffering ailments such as asthma and physical disabilities like cerebral palsy.

Ogendele (2020) reports on a recent study of children who became looked after and were referred to the health services. The study found the pre-school children aged 1 to 4 years to be the largest group diagnosed with behavioural and neurodevelopmental problems. The term 'disability' refers to a range of physical and sensory impairments and learning disabilities as well as to emotional and behavioural difficulties. Children with these problems still tend to be un der-represented in child protection statistics because their disability is mainly hidden. Yet these children's greater need for personal care and stimulation leaves them especially vulnerable.

Play that involves physical exercise helps young children to use their bodies and develop skills while enhancing their relationships with their caregivers.

Physical Development encompasses the following skills:

- Gross motor skills: rolling, sitting, crawling, walking, running and jumping.

- Fine motor skills: holding toys, manipulating objects such as transformer toys, posting shapes, threading, holding a pencil, operating scissors, or tweezers.

- Visual motor skills: what children do with items in their hands, such as colouring, cutting, putting together pieces of Duplo, Lego and so on.

- Speech-language and communication skills: early social smiling, recognising own name, babbling, talking, awareness of non-verbal expression of feelings.

- Feeding skills: drinking from a bottle or cup, eating a wide variety of age-appropriate foods with good chewing and swallowing, and simple meal preparation such as mixing biscuit dough, helping spread jam on bread.

- Adaptive play skills: learning how to play with toys, learning and doing imaginative play, and learning how to play with other children.

- Self-care skills: dressing, feeding, bathing and toileting.

Touch

The need for children to be able to tolerate touch is essential to their healthy development. After all, young children need to be bathed, fed, entertained and kept safe. Parents regularly pick up their child to remove them from harm such as burning fingers on a hot plate or running into a busy road. None of this protection is possible without touching the child. Consequently, as Norris and Rodwell (2017) point out, touch is the first 'language' that children learn. However, while touch can feel nurturing for children who are well looked after, for others it can feel very different, even threatening. Under-stimulated children chew their cuffs and break pencils by pressing them too hard. Sexually abused children develop a fear of textures such as glue and sand. However, some learn that touch is the only way to win attention and approval from adults. As a result of traumatic experience, children may dread having their hair washed or brushed, or hate the feel of certain fabrics or being tickled or touched accidentally. Poor early care can leave many children having immense problems with sensory experience.

Sensory integration

Sensory integration is the system by which the brain registers our reaction to a sensory stimulus and guides our response to it. For example, when we smell and taste a particular food we know if we want to eat it. Young children's brains can be less developed and less able to react as competently (see Glossary of Terms). Certain patterns of avoidance and coercion stem from the inability to interpret sensory information. Daily care activities or 'rough and tumble' play may overwhelm a child. Sensory experiences inhibit their states of arousal and affect their awareness of boundaries, consequences, space and time. This inhibited sense of awareness also impacts on their relationships with their family and peers. Lloyd (2016) helpfully identifies four systems in the brain involved in sensory awareness, which affect the trajectory of children's development:

The **limbic system** (emotional brain) is dependent on neural connections being made between it and other parts of the brain. Chronic, repeated neglect prevents connections being made (Gerhardt, 2004). Consequently, children who are less able to think act on impulse instead. It is confusing for them to be unable to identify physical feelings in their tummy, or on their skin. They may show irrational reactions to threats such as wasp stings or unfamiliar noise as they are less able to access their parasympathetic nervous system in order to self-calm.

The **vestibular system**, responsible for balance and coordination, develops the brain's sensory system. The neglected infant who has rarely been picked up or comforted – just 'parked' in front of the television for hours – may not have exercised muscles that allow his brain to coordinate its parts, therefore he is likely to be floppy and lack the core strength expected of his age.

The **proprioceptive system** controls groups of muscles, which enable us to do things like carry a drink without spilling it. The child with sensory delay may use far too much force to throw a ball, or might rush around bumping into furniture and trip over things, unable to adjust her strength. She may hurry too impulsively to anticipate, stop and work round obstacles. The child may lack concentration in performing basic tasks such as sitting down and follow even simple instructions.

The **tactile system** is for touch, which affects every area of the body and is essential for developing secure attachment. Children might flinch from touch, which for them feels scary, especially if they have been abused.

How play can help

Having fun and sharing emotional experience will help to build bonds between children and their caregivers. For children who have problems with sensory integration, an important benefit of play is that it enables the child to accept being touched through the safety of taking a role in which they act as 'someone else'. In a wedding scene, the couple hold hands to walk down the aisle. In the course of dancing, we would naturally brush against each other, just as in pirate play pirates joust and jostle each other. Similarly, a creative activity such as junk modelling allows the adult and child to touch each other as one holds pieces together while the other applies the tape, for example.

Key points

- Children's imagination develops in story making and creative play.

- In play, children advance in their physical development.

- By identifying the child's emotional age, caregivers can meet needs at the age being displayed.

Case examples
Rory, aged 2

At birth, Rory, the youngest of three children, needed help to breathe properly. Nurses noticed his learning-disabled mother didn't seem to know how much medicine to give him. She and the children lived with her father, the children's maternal grandfather. The children's father, also learning disabled, visited the family most days. Rory spent hours in his baby seat, stuck in a dark corner between two sofas, from which he leaned to peer out. His vision became so impaired he needed to wear glasses all the time but his mother often forgot to put them on him. Rory was delayed in learning to crawl and walk and was rarely heard vocalising. His nappies left unchanged for lengthy periods caused soreness and rashes. Social workers reported that the children were dressed in dirty clothes and the family home was 'indescribably filthy'. When the washing machine broke down, the grandfather couldn't afford to replace it. He refused to have the central heating on even in winter. Rory's mother didn't play with him because she had no idea how to play. She did not go to mother and baby groups, having no inkling of their value. It was her disclosure that the father was handling the children roughly that led to their coming into care.

HOW RORY'S FOSTER PARENT HELPED

Rory's foster carer encouraged him to climb up and down stairs, by supporting him from behind (as he ascended) and in front (for his descent). Regular exercise on a climbing frame and trampoline helped to advance Rory's mobility and build his muscle strength. The foster carer spent a lot of time talking to Rory and singing nursery rhymes and songs, which he loved. Being told stories about animals taken to a new family helped prepare Rory for his move to adoption. In play with toy animals in a sand tray he was able to practice what would happen when the adoptive parents came to see the children in their foster home. Rory was very excited when he visited his new home before moving in and made a successful transition to his new life.

Lola, aged 4

Lola, aged 4, and her sister, aged 6, witnessed violent fights between their birth parents. These parents had abusive childhoods and used alcohol and drugs as a means of coping. The birth mother attempted suicide then moved to another area to escape. A few months later she returned and persuaded the father to look after the children. Each parent accused the other of deceit over drug use. The ensuing violence led to the children's removal to foster care. The foster carer found Lola unable to dress or feed herself or use the toilet. Lola gave no clues as to when she was filling her nappy. She babbled, spoke only a handful of words and resisted physical contact. Assessments led to a diagnosis of 'global developmental delay' and subsequently, autism. Of particular concern was Lola's protracted screaming and poor sleep – problems that escalated after Lola met her new baby sister born to her birth mother, which was also upsetting for her older sister. Seeing herself as having been 'replaced' as the baby, Lola went on to suffer night terrors for weeks.

HOW GUIDED PLAY THERAPY HELPED

These night terrors reduced substantially over the course of regular weekly play therapy. Lola checked a 'baby's' (doll) heartbeat with a (toy) stethoscope. As she fed her dolls, changed their nappies and spread lotion on their limbs she gave these 'babies' the nurturing attention she craved for herself. Lola asked for help to tip water from a baby bottle into the potty. The therapist hesitated, aware that it could cause a mess and that Lola might be confused if allowed to do something not generally permitted. Her foster carer said, 'We don't normally fill a potty from a bottle' and asked Lola why she wanted to do this. Lola screamed. A bit later, Lola picked up a dolly's bottle containing water as though to drink it. The therapist gently said she could drink it if she wanted. As she brought the teat to her lips, Lola screamed again. The sensory experience of the teat in her mouth seemed to have triggered a traumatic memory. Lola then wrapped herself in a fleecy blanket and curled up to her foster carer.

In play with a toy TV, Lola repeatedly changed channels. She picked up a toy and pressed its talking button at least thirty times. Lola loved stories and asked for them to be reread multiple times. This repetitive play was her way of making sense of a world that confused her. In puppet play, her toys went on a 'picnic'. Lola picked up a toy guitar and sang to them joyfully.

Some weeks on, the therapist was asked to prepare Lola for a visit to her baby sister, whose presence had upset her so much. She and Lola looked at pictures of dolls of varying sizes. Lola came to realise that her little sister, who was still with their birth mother, would have grown bigger, also that this baby sister would not have all the treats she and her older sister were privilege to in their foster home.

Within a few weeks, Lola progressed to using 200 words, her vocabulary increasing all the time. Although her speech was indistinct her development had advanced to approximately 36 months. Lola still filled her nappy without telling her foster carer, but was now able to dress herself, to eat with a spoon and go up and down stairs unaided. Play had been significant in bringing on her development. Lola specially enjoyed finger painting, cutting, sticking and gluing, activities that developed her fine motor skills. She was calmer, more ready to trust and attach securely to her foster carer. Accordingly, the placement was subsequently confirmed as 'permanent'.

Activities
Trampoline

Children love to show off their newly acquired skills to an admiring audience so this exercise is exceptionally good for enhancing bonding and attachment.

On a trampoline (ideally one that has safety walls) invite the child to jump up and bounce to their feet from landing, somersault forward onto their knees, then get back up on their feet. Bounce with the child, holding their hands for encouragement and bonding.

ELG01: Listening and attention – from gaining the admiring adult's undivided attention, the child will become keener to listen and follow instructions. It helps the child used to being in control of adults to accept nurturing authority.

ELG04: Moving and handling – these exercises improves physical dexterity, control and coordination as the child moves, negotiating the space.

ELG06: Self-confidence and self-awareness – enabling children to have fun protects children's brains against the possible impact of depression and leads even traumatised children to gain more confidence and self-awareness.

'Please may I?' game

This is a game to encourage bonding as well as enhance movement skills. The adult gives instructions to the child such as *'Walk three steps towards me.'* The child then asks, *'Please may I?'* and follows the adult's instruction. The adult might direct the child to, for example, run, hop, rock, dance, jump, sit, roll, turn or skip. When the child reaches the parent/practitioner, she is given a hug. Try encouraging children by talking to them rather than by helping them physically, so as to give them the chance to try it out alone. It can be sometimes be fun to reverse roles.

ELG01: Listening and attention – the above-mentioned game develops the child's listening skills and their ability to follow instructions. It helps the child who is used to being in control of adults to accept nurturing authority.

ELG02: Understanding – this activity enables the child's sense of competence for exploring new activities and socialising. Attunement with the child's caregiver will increase in the course of fun and laughing together.

ELG04: Moving and handling – the 'Please may I?' game improves physical dexterity, control and coordination as the child moves, negotiating the space.

ELG06: Self-confidence and self-awareness – enabling traumatised children to have fun protects their brains against the possible impact of depression and leads them to gain confidence and self-awareness.

Animal Olympics

With hand puppets or soft toys, encourage the child to hold a contest called 'Animal Olympics'. The animal characters take part in competitions to see how high or how far they can jump, run or swim or dance. One character can be the compere announcing each act. The repetition of phrases as the race is announced and players are asked to line up at the starting line help to build new links in the child's brain. Some of the characters can be the 'judges'. It can lead to discussion on rules about what is fair or seen as cheating and how this should be dealt with, such as how many chances are allowed for someone claiming not to know the rules, including everyone starting at the same time, no pushing, etc.

EARLY LEARNING GOALS

ELG04: Moving and handling – the child learns from manipulating objects about what does or doesn't work, and how to find ways round problems.

ELG17: Being imaginative – the child uses imagination to build unusual structures and objects from which story making can evolve.

Water play

Encourage children to wash their toys and pour water between various receptacles of different sizes. Add bubbles for fun. This is relaxing, soothing play, which helps the child to overcome fears related to water such as being

sucked down a plughole, which are characteristic of young children. If the child is afraid of water (perhaps from having been scalded or held under water), have plenty of ice cubes which are solid to start with (so less like running water). Before the child realises it, he will be playing with the water after the ice has melted. Toy figures can also be added to the water tray. See the water game in Chapter 8 as a way to use water for building attachment security.

EARLY LEARNING GOALS

ELG04: Moving and handling – children learn to improve coordination.

ELG12: Shape, space and measures – in water play, children learn the relative proportions from how much each jug contains.

ELG17: Being imaginative – the child uses imagination to build unusual structures and objects, from which story-making can evolve.

Experimenting with sand

Pouring sand and adding water to it enables children to experiment with shapes, weight and texture in the course of burying and finding toys, which also leads into story-making. Access to a variety of toys and tools allows for the children's preferences. This might be to explore the sand's texture and properties, to play at hiding and finding, build sandcastles or create stories. For the latter purpose, it is helpful to have toy people of all generations, vehicles, houses, animals, fantasy figures, and items such as trolleys, fences, suitcases, buggies, etc.

EARLY LEARNING GOALS

ELG04: Moving and handling – the child discovers physical properties of sand.

ELG06: Self-confidence and self-awareness – is gained from storytelling.

ELG17: Being imaginative – this will expand the child's creativity and problem-solving abilities.

Junk modelling

Constructions made from junk materials can represent the rebuilding of the child's life and relationships, just as mess making may symbolise a reworking of the mess of the child's earlier life.

Provide a variety of cardboard and plastic boxes and containers, coloured paper, tissue, newspaper, tubes, egg boxes, split pins, string, stapler, masking tape, scissors, PVA glue, sticky tape, and collage materials, together with stickers, sequins and coloured glitter for decoration.

Encourage and help the child to make things such as rockets or racing cars, televisions, robots or washing machines. Pieces of card can be used to make a pair of shoes or boots. Have lengths of fabric to create 'scenery' for play that will develop spontaneously into storytelling (see Moore, 2014, for more ideas).

EARLY LEARNING GOALS

ELG04: Moving and handling – the child learns from manipulating objects about what does or doesn't work, and how to find ways round problems.

ELG17: Being imaginative – the child uses imagination to build unusual structures and objects, from which story creation can evolve.

Paper boats

Make a paper boat by folding a sheet of A4 paper in half. Then turn the top folded corners down into the centre to form a triangle. This should leave a half-inch of paper to fold upwards over the triangle to make the shape of a boat that has a central sail once the sides are pulled out. The boats can be sailed under bridges, in streams or in the bath. Hold a competition to see which boat is the fastest.

ELG04: Moving and handling – the child learns from manipulating objects, about what does or doesn't work, and how to find ways round problems.

ELG17: Being imaginative – the child uses imagination to build unusual structures and objects, from which story making can evolve.

Sensory play

Children often lose themselves in sensory play, which can involve substances listed in Chapter 1 and/or items used in Heuristic play – see Chapter 4. Invite the children to try 'this or this'. The very act of making simple choices can empower children, who have a poor sense of self and little experience of having their views and feelings admired and appreciated.

ELG01: Listening and attention – This activity encourages the child to listen to his caregiver when he needs help to formulate plans for making things

ELG04: Moving and handling – The child learns from manipulating objects, about what does or doesn't work, and how to find ways round problems.

ELG17: Being Imaginative – The child uses imagination to build unusual structures and objects, from which story making can evolve.

Guess the smell

To enhance children's sensory perception, have a range of items in lidded containers or in boxes

that have finger holes in the top. Invite children to close their eyes and guess the smell and what they are touching.

Some suggestions are: herbs, fresh grass, lavender, orange and lemon segments or peel, jelly, sand, rice, TCP, boiled sweets, toast, rose petals, bleach, coffee grains, paint, onions, baby wipes, children's shampoo, or baby lotion, after sun lotion, vinegar, fabric conditioner, play dough, etc. Invite the child to talk about what the smell reminds them of and whether they like it.

EARLY LEARNING GOALS

ELG01: Listening and attention – this activity encourages the child to listen to the caregiver and pay attention to their senses.

ELG02: Understanding – this activity enables the child's sense of competence on recognition of familiar smells. Children's attunement with their caregiver will increase in the course of fun and laughing together.

ELG06: Self-confidence and self-awareness is gained from storytelling

Scripts and strategies
Play at the child's level

Sit on the floor or at a low table beside the child to demonstrate your sincere interest in him or her. Observing the child closely will help you to recognise signals indicating any particular struggles the child has. If the child is regularly bumping into things and knocking them over, he or she may be struggling with simple motor actions and will benefit from regular practice.

Tell a problem-solving story

Some children (especially if they have had a lot of stress in their life) use their control over elimination or eating as this is the only control available to them when life feels highly unpredictable and anxiety provoking. In such cases, the child may be too terrified to open their bowels.

Elimination: To address this issue, try telling a story about a poo that takes a long time to find its way through a dark maze of tubes but eventually emerges into daylight, feeling joyful. Or the story could be about a little bear carrying a heavy load on his sleigh. When a friend helps take some items off his sleigh, Little Bear discovers that he feels as light as air!

You could encourage the child to use a play dough extractor tool to squeeze pieces of play dough into a sausage shape. This can psychologically invite movement in other body parts. Also, when the child is sitting on the toilet she can be encouraged to blow bubbles, as this will help counteract the holding in.

Fussy eating/ food refusal: A story for this situation could be about a puppy that can't find any food he likes so he stops eating and goes hungry. Eventually the puppy is rescued and learns to enjoy nice smells such as baking, which encourage him to eat. Tell the story and encourage the child to play out her own version and/or join you in baking and icing biscuits. See recipe in Chapter 9

Give reassurance

Reward children for their efforts and cooperation even if they make mistakes. Reassure them of your willingness to help them until they master the activity.

Simplify tasks

A child who has motor difficulties when undertaking a sequence of tasks such as pouring a drink, rinsing the cup, then placing it in the dishwasher, will need you to break these tasks down into small steps. A discrete way to achieve change is through play in which the child makes pretend food from play dough and holds 'parties' for their toys (or play dough people). These fun activities provide practice in tricky tasks. The child learns simpler steps that become more manageable with regular rehearsal within the safety and privacy of play.

Comment on the play

Pay close attention to what the child is doing as she plays and state what is happening in her story, '*Oh, so now she's going to bed! Will her mummy tuck her in? Does the little girl need her Teddy? Oh, so now she's getting up. Wow, I wonder what will happen next?*' This will help the child to become more self-aware and responsive. Children who are unused to this gentle adult attention may ignore your help at first. Be gently persistent until she responds to you even if she doesn't take up your ideas. Any response is better than none!

Allow child to play at a younger stage

Consider allowing the child who is delayed to spend time in play activities with children who are a bit younger than him (on the pretext of 'helping out'). Maintaining this playful relationship with the child will reduce his fear of his vulnerability and tantrums, as you convince him of your emotional availability.

Raise self-esteem

Early years practitioners could give young children a badge or sticker to remind staff members to smile and praise them: *'Aren't you walking nicely!' 'How lovely to see your smile!' What a beautiful picture you've made!'*

Perceptive problems

Try to make use of children's alternative senses to compensate for any problems they have such as in differentiating right from left or with tasks that involve hand-eye coordination. For example, when you are teaching the alphabet, invite the child to cut out the letters in textured wallpaper, and draw letters and numbers in the air, using their arm rather than just their fingers. Reading things out loud can also help to reinforce the visual input.

Facial expression

For children struggling to recognise emotions on faces, make a scrapbook of people (look particularly for pictures of famous people) to encompass a wide range of expressions. Invite the child to identify the emotion shown on each of these people's faces. Encourage the child to demonstrate the same expressions.

Learning about time

A way to help children to learn about time is by talking to them about what is going to happen next and how long it will take: *'In a minute I'm going to get dinner started, and you can play on your own for ten minutes. Then I'll join you.'* When the same event (such as a favourite TV programme that starts at 4pm and lasts for 30 minutes) repeats at the same time every day, the child will learn that when the programme starts, this means it is 4pm. She will also come to realise approximately how long the period of 30 minutes lasts. Some domino packs have different coloured dots for each number, for example, the 4s are yellow, 5s are blue and so on. This helps children learn their numbers, which they come to associate with the colour. With slightly older children try a game of 'Fives'. This involves placing pieces with dots adding to five next to the piece with a five. This game, involving 'fives' can also be used to convey to children that clock time is carved into five-minute sections to help them explore how long five minutes is as a route to learning about clock time.

7 Language and speech development

Introduction

The global rise in communication via text messaging and social media sites has been distracting many parents from taking time to talk to their children. This, along with the social isolation measures put in place to prevent the spread of COVID-19, has been compounding children's speech and language delay. Assessing the socio-emotional development in young children in the wake of social isolation, Urbina-Garcia (2020: 2) remarks that, 'Children's views are widely ignored by their parents'. If no one pays attention to the child's babble, the child will learn that she doesn't matter to anyone. Spending too much time watching television has often been blamed for poor development but research finds the picture to be more complicated than that. For example, much depends on the kind of programmes the child watches. Additionally, social isolation measures have limited young children's physical interaction and social opportunities to mix with their cousins, grandparents, friends, as well as their teachers and others from pre-school or school.

The strain of lockdown and the financial hardships following this raises the stress and anxiety levels in parents and accordingly their children. Delay in speech and language development is commonly linked with poor socio-economic backgrounds and parents with a low level of education. Subjection to neglect and abuse leaves many children growing up to believe that they are unworthy of attention. As a consequence of inadequate attention and an inability to express themselves verbally, children have less self-control and hence are observed to be showing greater frustration and aggression (Clarke et al, 2020).

This chapter proposes ways to create opportunities to listen to children and engage them in play activities so that interactions taking place between parents or practitioners and the children improve, and the children's cognitive, social and emotional wellbeing is promoted and enhanced.

The effect of language and speech delay

Children who understand little of what adults around them are saying may call an object by a wrong name or quickly forget any new words they have learned. They might hear the first part of the sentence and miss the rest of it. They may jumble sentences or stutter and stammer. Impediments such as these affect children's confidence in speaking. As a result of severe anxiety, some children develop tics associated with Tourette's Syndrome. Communication and language are central to learning and relationships. In recognition of this, Makaton has been developed as a sign and symbol language to help those with difficulties in communication and learning. Several early years settings are adopting the language of Makaton and are becoming accredited to a talking scheme organised by Ican www.ican.org.uk to help children with their communication skills.

Warning signs of speech and language delay
The child:

- Shows little interest in communicating and talks especially slowly.

- Makes speech or language sounds that are unusual for her age.

- Sounds muddled and has difficulty in organising thoughts into words or in telling you about something that happened.

- Has difficulty locating a word that she remembers at other times.

- Does not respond to sounds, or appear to understand simple instructions or requests, and does not feel understood.

- Fails to pay attention to things that adults point to and talk about.

- Struggles to keep friends, join in games with older children, understand jokes, or keep up with conversations.

Key points

- Allow the child to express him or herself according to the age he or she is displaying. Children move on when they are ready.

- Take the children's cues and check with them how the role is to be played, what they think should happen, and what might then result.

- Seeing change occur in play enables children to realise that they can transfer the same powers – for example, of reasoning – to day-to-day life.

Case examples

Naomi, aged 4

Naomi was three years old when she was placed in foster care with her younger brother and sister, following chronic neglect and domestic violence in their family of origin. Advanced tooth decay and inflammation from head lice had left Naomi's mouth and scalp very sore. A year later the children moved to their adoptive family. Soon after that, a gang killed their birth parents. Naomi had night terrors until she was enabled to process her fears in play.

HOW NAOMI'S ADOPTIVE MOTHER HELPED

Naomi struggled to know who she was or how to 'be'. In her play with toy animals, she began to enact a story that started on a 'dark night' and then progressed on to a 'sunny day'. In the story a tortoise wonders whether anyone can be trusted and finds its way to a park where there is a princess who *'keeps her crown on.'* Possibly, the princess needed this reassurance of her identity. Alternatively, the crown may have been a symbol of protection.

Naomi moved on to play with baby dolls. Bathing and smothering them in lotion, she began to recover nurture. Naomi then asked her adoptive mother to act as her baby. As they cuddled together, Naomi realised that she wanted to be the baby herself. Being wrapped in a fleece and cradled was an experience that Naomi enjoyed very much. A few days later, while lying in her mother's arms, Naomi threw a toy rattle, which her mother retrieved and gave back to her – a sequence that repeated several times and was reminiscent of the 8 to 12 months stage. The following week, Naomi chose to sit in her (baby) sister's high chair, but on the next occasion, on being asked where she wanted to sit, she announced, *'I'm not a baby!'* and sat on a 'grown up' chair, stating she was ready for play with clay and making stories. Naomi had used the privacy of play to move through developmental stages and recover missed nurture. As she gained a sense of security, her night terrors ceased.

TJ, aged 4

TJ was two years old when he was removed from his family of origin due to neglect, parents' alcohol abuse, mental ill health and domestic violence. TJ had already moved three times within his extended birth family. He went on to have four foster placements before being placed in his adoptive family, aged four, with his sister aged two. A highly insecure child, TJ appeased adults to win approval, but showed very limited ability for imaginative play. An outcome of his mother's heavy drinking throughout pregnancy was that TJ had poor motor control for tasks such as using scissors, threading beads or cleaning his teeth. Nevertheless, he was a cheerful and generous natured child who was protective of his younger sister and adored dressing up for 'hero' play.

HOW GUIDED PLAY THERAPY HELPED

Attracted to the doll's house, TJ soon had lots of *visitors* ring its doorbell. The *mother* invited each of these callers to come in for a 'cup of tea'. This led to *tea parties* and the *children* then going to the *park* with their new friends. TJ's stories also featured regular *accidents* such as children 'falling out of bed.' On one occasion the arrival of 'Army soldiers' made the house overcrowded. The soldiers were told to leave but they stayed and many died in the ensuing battle. The play enabled TJ to process his early memories of life in very overcrowded accommodation and of unwelcome visitors causing his world to change. He surmised that survival was merely a lottery.

In another of his plays, Elephant (therapist) trumpeted crossly. PC Plod (TJ) told Elephant off. *'You must stop making those rude noises!'* On repeating the noises Elephant was led away. As far as TJ was concerned, cross feelings were not allowed and must be repressed and anyone expressing them gets locked up. TJ sensed that he was undeserving of kindness and not entitled to negative feelings. His underlying insecurity was apparent in his story about Penguin, whose mixed-up feelings prompted him to be aggressive. TJ agreed to let Penguin go to a 'safe place' until he felt ready to make friends.

Soon after TJ moved to his adoptive family, the strain he felt under became evident as he had Elephant repeatedly bash at the door (of the doll's house). When things broke, he admitted he *'didn't feel like saying sorry!'* The therapist's reflection that Elephant could not explain why he felt this way prompted his adoptive mum to say, *'Elephant obviously needs a home!'* Accepting the offer, TJ declared he felt safe and welcome in this house.

On one occasion, TJ took the role of a 'brave boy' and cast the therapist as a 'Witch', directing her to act nasty. Non-verbal signals were agreed for showing if either became 'injured' or 'dead'. Finding her spells to be ineffectual, the Witch asked, *'How can I be evil if my spells don't work?'* TJ as 'brave boy' replied, *'You could try being good for a change!'* The Witch asked how she could be good. TJ advised her to take off her hat. Now that she was 'good', the Witch granted the 'brave boy' three wishes. He asked for a magic carpet ride, the removal of weapons and to be rid of evil. Seeing such transformation occur within the play helped TJ realise that change also happened in real life, and that by using his imagination he was able to resolve all sorts of problems.

Activities
Dramatic play

Invite the child to join you on a tour of discovery. Aim to combine lots of movements and actions. Follow the child's lead, but if the child can't think where to start, have a couple of ideas ready for her to choose from. (More than two choices may be too difficult for her to manage.) The drama might involve use of swords (see Chapter 3, Sword dances, for guidance) for slaying sharks or pirates competing for territory. Encourage the child to decide what dangers she might encounter and help her to plan how to work as a team so that the threat of danger will be

overcome. Through this interaction you are sharing information. You will also excite the child who without this connection with you may get lost in her own thoughts. To ensure a balance and provide psychological comfort, have the characters discover exciting food on their journey, such as toffee apple trees and candyfloss bushes. When the story reaches a natural break, older children might like to paint a picture of the scene or sculpt it. Sculpting (see Glossary) is a dramatic device which involves the players in creating a sculpture by bending each other's bodies into various shapes to show how the characters felt at various stages in the play.

Caution: Maintain safe boundaries: for example, if in a dark room keep the lights on (even if the child wants them switched off); be careful about where you touch a child who is highly anxious about physical proximity of adults, even though the context of play usually lends the safety of fictional distance.

'Strictly Come Dancing'

Lots of young children love this TV programme. In guided play, they can take turns with the adults as dancers and being a judge. The child acting as the famous judge Craig Revel Horwood might adopt his phrases: *'Three words – I loved it!' 'A – maz – ing!' 'Fab – u – lous!'' 'Cha, Cha, Cha!'* or *'Very stompy, darling!' 'Your hands were splayed!' 'There was no hip action!'* and *'It was a dis-aster darling!'*

The repetition of these phrases will invite fun and laughter and enhance the child's speech and language development.

EARLY LEARNING GOALS

ELG03: Speaking – dramatic play enables children to expand their vocabulary, for both verbal and non-verbal (emotional) expression.

ELG06: Self-confidence and self-awareness – this increases via having fun, and expanding self-expression in cooperative play.

ELG17: Being imaginative – children learn to use their imagination in original ways and gain confidence

Stories, jokes and rhymes

By sharing stories, jokes and rhymes that children are likely to enjoy, you enable them to pick up subliminal messages, take courage from the heroes and learn from this fictional experience. For children, who are delayed in language development, repeat their favourite stories to them as many times as you can. Exaggerating and slowing down your delivery of the stories and rhymes will give the child more chances to notice and learn the sounds and meanings.

Libraries have lots of stories for children who have undergone changes in their lives. Coram-BAAF supply books on issues typically faced (such as poor sleep, food refusal, and hoarding). These stories illustrate resolutions that the child may not have considered and in the privacy of fiction, discretely give the child much needed reassurance.

ELG17: Being imaginative – Reading stories stretches children's imagination. Stories that are solution focussed will develop children's ideas about how to resolve their own feelings and problems.

Naming songs

Make up a song about the child's name, and its meaning (which you can google). This will help the child learn about their identity and talk about how important this is to him or her. It also replicates the early parent-infant attachment dance, and helps vulnerable children to feel more secure.

ELG06: Self-confidence and self-awareness – this exercise helps the child to develop a positive sense of self. For children in new families, it reinforces the sense of identity as a member of this family. Children will have more enthusiasm for learning if feeling secure in attachment relationships.

ELG08: Making relationships – this exercise helps children to process grief, and appreciate who in their life is most important to them.

Creative visualisation and painting

This is a valuable activity both for stimulating children's imagination and finding out about their wishes and feelings they may not have shared with you, but which are about the people they worry about

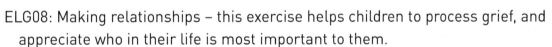

or wish they could see. To invite creative visualisation, you might use the following script:

> *You are in a warm, cosy room. The window opens and a magical rug comes in and lands on the floor. As you sit on this magical rug, a wind lifts you up and out of the window. You sail up into the sky, over rooftops and hills. Now you see a basket of delicious food appear in front of you. Each time you eat something, another yummier treat appears. After a while, you have a nap. When you wake up, you're in front of a door. Who do you see?*

Invite the child to draw or paint who they see. When a child has undergone several changes of care, the person they depict often reveals which attachment figure they are missing the most. Acknowledging the child's feelings is vital to helping them to grieve their painful loss.

EARLY LEARNING GOALS

ELG08: Making relationships – this exercise helps children to process grief, and appreciate who in their life is most important to them.

ELG17: Being imaginative – this activity also expands their imagination.

Telephone conversations

Two toy phones are ideal for you and the child to chat with. Or you can hold your hand to your ear and pretend to talk into a phone. Ideally allow the child to lead the conversation but if she is shy or unsure how to do this, show her. Start by talking about things that are familiar to the child: For example, pretend to phone the local shop to find out if it is open and ask for 'rainbow sweets' or the child's favourite cereal.

Then 'phone' the other parent to ask what time they will be home. Then pass the phone to the child and say, *'Daddy/Mummy wants to know if you'll play with them when they get home.'* Make a pretend call to pre-school and ask the teacher how the child is getting on: *'Is she happy?'*, *'Has she got friends?'*, *'Does she like it there?'* Ask the child what she thinks the teacher will say. Invite the child to be 'teacher' and say what she thinks about the child.

This is a useful technique for exploring how the child is feeling, and if there is someone she is missing. You might pretend to phone the last foster parent to ask how she/he is getting on without the child. Encourage the child to reply in this role. You could phone Spiderman or Wonder Woman, to ask what they might do in a predicament. Get the child to respond in the hero role.

EARLY LEARNING GOALS

ELG02: Understanding – children realise that their feelings are understood

ELG03: Speaking – children explore their ideas and beliefs and have them reflected back by the attendant adult.

ELG15: Technology – children understand and express their thoughts and feelings in imaginative dramatic play, in which their stories soon emerge.

Games

(1) 'SIMON SAYS'

Some children do not understand all the words that adults use. This game allows the adult to observe how well a child is able to follow more than one instruction at a time, such as *'put your hand on your head and touch your side'*. Try adding, *'touch your nose.'* If the child cannot do this easily, he or she may soon drift to a different activity.

Give the child one brief instruction at a time and admire their talents in other areas. If the child drifts off, engage them in imaginative play about a superhero, such as Batman or Wonder Woman, and suggest a character that needs to be rescued.

(2) 'I SPY WITH MY LITTLE EYE'

This game will enhance the child's observational and language skills. You will encourage bonding via praising the child when they make a correct guess.

If the child is not ready to play the traditional version of *'I spy something beginning with* [say] *S'*, instead say *'I spy something the colour of ...'*

EARLY LEARNING GOALS

ELG01: Listening and attention – this game gives children practice at listening and expressing their own ideas and thoughts.

ELG02: Understanding – the child will learn to understand new words, phrases and concepts.

ELG03: Speaking – the child will develop vocal skills from joining in.

Scripts and strategies

Supporting dramatic play

Dramatic play is a far more fun way for young children to practice speaking and listening than in structured lessons. Playing out events such as parties, weddings or, say, arguments between two characters such as Spiderman and Optimus Prime, or Cinderella's stepsisters, provide excellent opportunities for learning since children will experiment spontaneously. You, the adult playmate, can help out the child who is having trouble with particular sounds by using phrases with that sound or incorporating that sound into a character's name.

If you try to give too many complicated instructions, it can provoke a negative reaction from the child who is struggling with receptive language. Instead, keep to giving simple suggestions one at a time. You might make a theatrical aside, such as, *'We need to make this place safe!'* Then in role as the 'baddy', suggest, *'How about I break out of jail – you fetch a police officer!'* When the baddie is caught, you then ask, *'What's going to happen next?'*

Talking corner

Have a talking corner – in pre-school, this can be in a part of the room that has comfortable seating, where children can sit together to chat and be encouraged to sort out any disagreements. At home, a comfy chair can be the designated place for regular chats about feelings and for explaining things that puzzle the young child, who is asking lots of 'why?' questions.

Check level of understanding

All children mature at different rates. Some are better at decoding words and sounds; others are more skilled at deciphering what they see. Some children have difficulty with understanding things, but are adept at masking this problem by having an apparently remarkable ability to express complex ideas using their imagination. A child who ignores the adult's suggestions may not realise or see the relevance of them. When the child does not respond as expected, she may not have understood what is wanted of her. It is easy to assume she is being belligerent or stubborn. Before you do, check that she has properly understood the words you have used and their meaning. Try a game of 'Simon Says' (see above). If the child disengages, it is most likely he or she is not able to understand or follow the instruction. It will be important to try a different activity or simplify the game by reverting back to giving a fun instruction that the child understands in order to re-engage her.

Eye contact

When giving instructions, look the child in the eyes and speak calmly. However, be aware that for traumatised children, eye contact can feel especially stressful. It can make them fearful of being hit or disappointing you and feeling shamed. The child who is especially anxious might not know the words you are using, or may be too hypervigilant to his surroundings to listen to you. You can check the child has understood by asking him gently to repeat what you said and to say what he thinks you meant. Think how to help him to better understand things.

Make use of meal times

Put phones on silent and out of reach during meals and have television turned off to convey to children how much it matters to pay close attention to conversation. Talk to the children about what is going on for them, and prepare them for plans for the rest of the day. It is especially valuable for children to have meals at the table with their caregiving parents and/or the adults in the pre-school setting. The children learn table manners and how to conduct themselves from being given undivided attention with no distractions.

Singing and rhymes

There is a wealth of songs and nursery rhymes which can be sung in pre-school or around the house while preparing meals, or doing jobs such as gardening, or while in the car on journeys to school, holidays, etc. Singing and chanting familiar rhymes will enhance children's development, give them a sense of belonging and ability to enjoy fun in the devoted adult's company.

8 Separation and loss

Introduction

The devastating impact of loss for babies and young children separated from their primary attachment figure has been extensively written about, most notably by Bowlby (2007) and Fahlberg (1994). Children need explanations and leading evidence-based practice advises us to put the 'unspeakable' into words (Lieberman et al, 2015). Yet, as Eyre et al (2020) note, when the child asks *'Where's Daddy?'*, the communications about what has happened and where Daddy has gone do not always match the tone and facial expressions which accompany the content being delivered. The parents' emotional experience inevitably influences their version of events. The confusion that results for children can get embedded in their implicit memory.

Consequences of separation and loss

For children removed from birth parents' care, a consequence can be the loss of stories, rituals, customs and memories of their life in their birth family. The trauma caused by the loss of important relationships following this separation is further exacerbated when multiple changes of caregiver ensue. Triseliotis (2002) found key factors affecting children's ability to adjust well in the long term were the age at which they get placed, and being placed in a stable family, rather than undergoing frequent changes of placement. Whether the child is with a sibling or placed separately will have an influence and some children have far greater resilience than others, although there are no clear explanations as to why.

Signs of anxiety to watch out for in children include regression in toileting, aggression, clinging and/or seeking of inappropriate physical contact, often rooted in a craving for comfort. The distressed child might refuse to let the caregiver dress or undress her. She may refuse to eat or to use the potty or toilet. Resistant to the new stranger charged with caring for her, the child might cry and throw herself on the floor, yet refuse to be picked up and comforted. Bedtimes can be especially difficult if she is unable to tolerate being left or panics when a caregiver perceived as a stranger enters the room. She may cry at a frightening pitch, alerting neighbours to her extreme distress.

Recognising grief

The involved adults need to recognise what young children's behaviour and actions are communicating about their experiences and put this into words for them. 'Basic trust' (Erikson, 1950) comes with the sense of feeling safe and belonging. However, when children move to new situations, whether this is to a stepparent, relatives, friends, foster care or adoption, there is an expectation on the child to forget about the past in case this makes it too hard for them to move forward and form a secure attachment to their new family. Some adoptive or foster parents, highly anxious about the children being too attached to the former parents, cease to allow the children to have contact with their former carers more abruptly than is helpful for the children.. Children need time to adjust their allegiances and as Lanyado (2003) points out, often need to grieve the loss of the former parents to whom they were attached. Some will not have been enabled to grieve previous losses of birth family, friends or pets. In my experience, once the new parents fully accept their children's feelings and allow visits with the people most important to them, the children eventually come to accept their losses and attach more securely to their new parents.

Play enables the grieving process.

This grieving process is necessary, and the safest way to facilitate it is via creative and imaginative play, in which the children practice their impending moves and explore their history. In the play context, as they make sense of 'what happened', children are free to process their intense feelings of anger, frustration and abandonment instead of acting these feelings out in everyday life. Weber and Haen (2005) remark that once children realise that even their foster, kinship or adoptive parents can be 'good enough' (Winnicott, 1965) they will feel more encouraged to experiment with their changing identity.

Key Points

- Telling stories that parallel the child's experience help the child to sense his experiences have been understood and to learn empathy for himself.

- Stories that solve problems encourage children to use the same skills for situations in real life.

- It is most important to acknowledge the feelings arising in the play.

Case examples

Amela, aged 4

Amela had been placed for adoption from foster care. In her birth family, she witnessed domestic violence and substance addiction, this being her parents' way of getting by following abuse in their own childhoods. The adoptive parents worried that Amela showed no recognition of their parental authority. She was dismissive towards them, treating them as her peers. Amela's frequent requests to see her last foster carer compounded their anxiety. They tried to show her a picture of her birth mother as a way of starting the conversation about why she was living with them but Amela refused to look at it. She was having nightmares that she couldn't explain, was approaching strangers for attention, and showing more interest in food than in her new parents, who had become immensely anxious about the child's ability to attach to them.

HOW GUIDED PLAY THERAPY HELPED

Sensing that Amela was feeling alienated, the therapist told her a story about a brave princess being rescued from her cruel father and taken to a new place where everything feels strange and different. On showing Amela the life map drawn for her, the therapist remarked on how lucky Amela was to be chosen. Amela shrank from her. However, as events from her life were played out, she began to recall memories and through her stories reveal that she had felt 'kidnapped'. Amela loved hopscotch so the therapist told her a story about a sad bunny going to a new rabbit family and learning hopscotch (see *Hopscotch*, Appendix 5, Story 2). Amela and her adoptive mother then played hopscotch on the patio. Amela began to reconcile to life in her new family. The therapist retold her life story using the water game (see Activities). Amela enjoyed filling the parent jugs with 'love' and having them reciprocate. In response to a story *Eddie the Eagle makes Friends* (Corrigan and Moore, 2011), Amela played out her own story about a young giraffe needing its mummy's help to make friends. She then transformed the room into a 'royal palace' and in the emerging play, practiced coping with separation. It culminated in Amela announcing in the sixth guided play session, '*My birth mummy couldn't look after me. They (social workers) tried to help. Then I grew big and my foster carer let me be adopted.*'

Toby, aged 4

Toby and his sisters (aged 5 and 2 years) had witnessed their birth parents' drug and alcohol addiction, from which their mother died. An aunt and uncle took the children in but neglected them. They were then taken to foster care with a plan for adoption. Unfortunately, during introductions to the adoptive family, the foster carer made it very difficult for the children to separate from her. Soon after they moved to their adoptive home, a gang killed their birth father. This led to months of sleep disturbance for the adoptive family. Toby was hypervigilant, and scared to sleep. Each night he was making noises that kept him, his siblings and exhausted adoptive parents awake for hours.

HOW TOBY'S ADOPTIVE PARENT HELPED

As Toby filled a small sand tray with toy people, he announced that most of the people were 'good' but some were 'bad'. His Power Rangers helped the goodies win their battles. However, these heroes had to keep taking a rest (the battles exhausted them, as occurs in real life). As the heroes lay down to rest Toby stiffened, saying *'They saw an angry man'*. Through the voice of the Power Ranger, his adoptive mum reflected, *'It's not good to be angry! It makes you even more tired!'* Toby proceeded to have Spiderman climb his web to keep watch over the forest, therein demonstrating his own desire to look after everyone. In the course of playing 'shops', Toby noticed goods being taken unpaid for. He phoned the 'police' then declared the shop was on fire so he called the 'fire brigade' as well. Subsequently Toby took the role of 'pirate', slayed a lion monster and rescued a 'mermaid' (Mum). At this point he chose to be a 'lamb' and snuggled cosily into the arms of his mummy 'sheep'.

To address Toby's fears, Mum read him a story about a dragon that turns out to be scared of mice. On meeting a lonely mouse called George, the dragon flees. The villagers hail George as a hero and from then on, he is never lonely again. Toby enjoyed more stories of heroes conquering their fears. Six weeks later he was sleeping through the night. Recovering nurture and having his fears validated led Toby to reframe his identity to one of a heroic survivor.

Activities
Identity tree (Moore, 2020)
This activity helps children to make links between their physical feelings and the emotional expression of them, and to gain control over their affect (see Glossary).

Part 1: Play rainforest music and pretend to be a 'tree' through the seasons. Invite the child to join you standing tall, spreading arms, as new leaves 'sprout' in spring. The child pictured is wearing big gloves to show big branches. The child might like to be a lamb and spring around your adult 'tree'. In the summer 'trees' grow heavy with leaves and fruit, providing shade for picnicking families. In the autumn, fruit is harvested and leaves drop. Trees bend under winter storms. Discuss which trees keep their leaves and which shed them. In 'winter' share (imaginary) gifts.

Part 2: Invite the child to lie along the length of a piece of plain wallpaper on the floor with his arms spread out but keeping his feet together (to represent the trunk). Draw round him, to make the outline of the 'identity tree'. The child can draw his hair and facial features onto the outline. Suggest he draw a heart on the part of the body where he feels love. Talk about other feelings we have and encourage him to show you where these might be felt on the body. For example, tears in the eyes, lump in the throat would suggest sadness. For excitement, or anxiety, suggest a knot where the tummy is.

Part 3: For older children, write on card leaves (you cut out in advance) all the positive words you can think of to describe them, e.g. lovely, clever, arty, kind, sporty, singer, friendly, brave, thoughtful, good at skipping. Help them attach these leaves to the 'tree' (using a glue stick). Provide fabrics of varying texture to cut out leaves and staple them to the tree. Ask the child what he likes about the fabrics he has chosen. Hang up the finished, colourful identity tree.

EARLY LEARNING GOAL

ELG06: Self-confidence and self-awareness – this exercise develops self-expression. The child connects their emotions with their physical feelings and gains confidence from having their positive attributes reinforced. Children become aware of their body via physical movement and dancing to music.

Hero painting

Hero paintings can be exceptionally enhancing for children, who lack belief in their right to voice their feelings. Provide a range of paint colours, ideally including gold and silver. Invite the child to create a picture of a brave hero. If he lacks confidence in

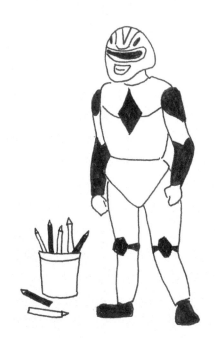

drawing, offer to draw the outline. The child can add features, such as sequins or buttons for eyes, silver or gold foil for the body, red felt for a cloak.

Help the child to make a 'superhero' mask and invite him to wear it for acting a play. Speaking from behind the mask will help him gain more confidence in talking like a hero. Ask the child what a hero is. If he doesn't know, tell him that heroes are brave and strong and that in stories, heroes such as Spiderman, Optimus Prime and Power Rangers frequently rescue people in difficulties.

Remind the child that he is a hero for having coped with lots of changes, often without help. Help him realise just how brave he had to be. Talk about why the hero needs a voice – to say what he thinks, to shout if he needs help, to sing songs – and why he needs to eat to keep strong and cry to show when he is upset. Depending on the child's level of understanding, you might write the hero's qualities next to the hero figure to reinforce his self-esteem. He may then feel encouraged to talk about times when he felt (or feels) unsafe. It is an opportunity to reinforce how much better life is for the child when he is being cared for properly.

EARLY LEARNING GOALS

ELG06: Self-confidence and self-awareness – children gain self-confidence and self-awareness on having their positive attributes reinforced

ELG07: Managing feelings and behaviour – this exercise enables children to ask 'how' and 'why' questions. The child can say when they do or don't need help, and be encouraged to talk about feelings concerning events in their life.

ELG13: People and communities – this exercise will be especially helpful for children who have moved to different families to recognise similarities and differences in the families they have lived in.

ELG16: Exploring and using media and materials – this activity increases confidence to choose resources and experiment with a variety of materials and tools.

Water game

SCRIPT FOR FOSTER/ADOPTIVE FAMILIES

This activity (called 'Loving Water' in Corrigan and Moore, 2011) was designed to help foster and adoptive families, who

have full background information about the child's life history. It is a way of helping the children to understand how they came to be living in this family.

Warm water represents feelings of loving kindness, and cling film is used as a symbol for 'hurt' that blocks the flow of positive, loving feelings. Have (ideally lightweight and transparent) jugs for 'parents' and cups to represent 'children'. Before you start, spread towels on the children's laps and beneath the large (washing up size) bowl of warm water placed on the table or floor. Have a roll of cling film and several pieces cut ready in advance to save time.

Ask the children if they would like to hear a story about why they are living with you. Children are usually intrigued enough to agree to this but you need their assent to continue. If the child refuses and their problems worsen, seek professional help. I often start the story by explaining that we are born of love, which is like warm water that flows until something happens to block it. (It is complicated if the child is born of rape, but under-fives are too young to be told about this.) We all like to feel we have been wanted, whatever happened. The following example can be adapted to fit your child's situation:

Part 1

Explain, '*This jug is the Daddy and this one is the Mummy*'. As you pour water from one jug to the other say, '*When Daddy met Mummy, he admired her pretty hair and she said to Daddy "You have nice eyes!" They filled each other with loving feelings and guess what happened?*' (The child often guesses that a baby came). Add a cup to the bowl. '*Yes, they made a baby, called....* [Invite child to say who]. *The baby was so cute and filled the parent with loving feelings.*' If the child has siblings, say: '*Mummy was so thrilled with this baby that she had another, called...* [child names each baby]'.

Part 2

'*Sadly, when this mummy and daddy were little, no one loved them enough so they didn't know how to look after babies*'. Wrap cling film over the parent jugs. '*They got upset and angry*'. Offer an explanation of the circumstances, for example:: '*They took pills and drank stuff that made them happy at first but then it made them very sick*'. Scripts for alternative circumstances are listed in the predicaments section. Add another layer of cling film over the parent jugs. '*They got too tired to look after their children and they kept saying it was the other one's turn to change the baby's nappy and make dinner*'. Clash the jugs so that water spills out. Some water will spill from parent jugs as they clash because it's difficult for them to remain sealed with clingfilm when immersed in water. Place cling film over the children's cups and explain: 'These are the hurting skins that came when the children cried but no one listened. More scary things happened, the children felt hungry and wore dirty clothes'. Add more cling film onto the 'children' cups. 'The social worker tried to help but the mummy thought they were just telling her off'. Place another layer of cling film on her cup. Explain that the children are safe now and invite them to punch their finger in the cling film on their cup, to allow water to be poured in or out.

Part 3

Explain that now the children are with you, they don't need these hurting skins any more. The cling film is removed from the children's cups, ceremoniously. The parent jugs now fill the children's cups until they are overflowing. Invite the children to fill your jugs in a continuous shared pouring of 'loving feelings'.

You might then suggest to the child that if at any time in the future he is feeling sad, he can put a cup of water in a place (such as the windowsill) that you will notice and know that it means he wants a cuddle.

Predicaments

Incarceration: If a parent is in prison, explain that prison is a 'time out' place for grown-ups, who have not followed the rules we all live by to keep safe.

Sexual abuse: If the child was sexually abused, explain that this abuser was still like a young child so used her as a doll and played with her in a wrong way. Say this person knew it was wrong but didn't understand about feelings.

Mental illness: If the birth parent is mentally ill, explain, 'Your first mummy's brain is poorly. She needs doctors in a special hospital to make her better'.

Learning disability: To explain this predicament, say, 'Your mummy/daddy didn't learn quickly. Social workers tried to teach them but they needed to have someone to copy all the time or they forgot what to do to look after children.'

SCRIPT FOR EARLY YEARS PRACTITIONERS

Early years practitioners are unlikely to have access to the family history of the children in their charge. It is important not to convey incorrect information. Even so, when troubled children are struggling to cope with changes in their situation, they can be helped to explore their feelings via the following script.

Have a (washing up size) bowl of warm water and prepare as for adoptive parents/foster carers. Explain, *'This warm water is like loving feelings that flow as long as we carry on being nice to each other. Look how people can fill each other up with love.'* Demonstrate pouring water between jugs. Ask, *'Would you like to have a go?'* You could give examples of nice things that people say to each other. *'I like your eyes!'*, *'Your hair is beautiful!'* Then ask, *'Shall I tell you a story?'*

If the child wants to hear your story, explain, *'Sometimes loving feelings get blocked when grown-ups do and say things to hurt and upset each other. Let's see how this happens'.* Wrap a sheet of cling film over the jugs. *'Look, now no love can get in or out!'* Show how the water is blocked from pouring either way. Then explain, *'Everyone wants to be loved, and when parents have children, they very much want to love them and look after them.'*

Place a cup (child) into the bowl and ask, *'What name shall we give this one?'* The child is likely to give it his/her name. Explain: *'When this baby was born, mummy thought he was perfect and gorgeous. She admired his tiny hands and feet and the folds in his elbows!'* Invite the child to think of things babies need, like to be picked up when they cry, to be fed, clean, nappy changed, talked to, etc. Explain: *'We can guess things were hard for Mummy (or Daddy) so she (or he) struggled to cope with upsetting feelings. When hurt feelings are bottled up, they often burst out. Now you're safe, let's see how much fun we can have.'* Make a plan with the child for enjoying their time in pre-school.

EARLY LEARNING GOALS

ELG01: Listening and attention – as children listen to stories they anticipate the key event and understand how stories evolve.

ELG03: Speaking – children express thoughts and feelings and tell their own stories and narratives.

ELG06: Self-confidence and self-awareness – are gained from talking about their ideas.

ELG07: Managing feelings and behaviour – children learn to adjust their behaviour to different situations, take changes of routine in their stride.

ELG08: Making relationships – from learning about their life story, children are better able to develop relationships with both adults and other children.

Stories about loss

When children learn the facts of their life story in a way that is meaningful for them, they will sense that their caregiving parents are being open with them. The children will cease to blame themselves and attach more securely to their new parents. Stories about equivalent predicaments can help to show that the outcome for the children will be a 'happy ending'.

Steps to story making:

1. Tell the stories about loss and separation. Read the stories *Enry Elf* or *Hopscotch* (Appendix 5, Stories 1 and 2) and/or create a story about loss and separation to share with the child. Have a hopeful outcome.

2. Discuss feelings arising in the story.

3. Encourage children to enact the story and develop their own story with toys, puppets and/or sensory materials such as clay, play dough and sand.

4. The story emerging in play will give you clues about how he experienced the story you shared and the connections he made to his own memories.

EARLY LEARNING GOALS

ELG01: Listening and attention – on listening to stories children anticipate the key event and understand how stories evolve.

ELG03: Speaking – children express thoughts and feelings and tell stories.

ELG06: Self-confidence and self-awareness – are gained from Enri talking about their ideas.

ELG07: Managing feelings and behaviour – children learn to adjust their behaviour to different situations, take changes of routine in their stride.

ELG08: Making relationships – from processing their losses, children develop better relationships with both adults and other children.

ELG17: Being imaginative – dramatic play encourages imagination.

Puppets expressing feelings

Puppets are ideal for chatting about feelings. Through the voice of the puppet, children practice ways to get support, solve problems, and sustain friendships. Animal puppets are especially effective for the under-fives. A puppet the child relates to can sit alongside her and give opinions in the course of play. During the water game described earlier, I often bring my monkey puppet, Monty, who I ask, *'What do you think of that? Did it make you sad that the baby's nappy wasn't changed and made him so sore he kept crying?'* I have Monty whisper in my ear that this really upset him and he can't believe how brave the child is. Puppets can share worries about losses and changes (see Chapter 9), and about what they believe others think of them.

Children often respond more easily to a puppet than to questions from an adult. Puppets can express and validate real feelings, yet in the context of play, sensitive and embarrassing issues (such as wetting and soiling) can be addressed in the privacy of the play being about 'someone else'. The child can deal with his worries by giving the puppet the reassurance he needs. In this way he finds hope, encouragement and new ways forward.

EARLY LEARNING GOALS

ELG02: Understanding – on hearing stories about the experiences of the puppet character, children ask questions and gain deeper understanding.

ELG03: Speaking – children express their thoughts and feelings through developing their own narratives and responding to feelings being expressed.

ELG06: Self-confidence and self-awareness – from hearing the puppet validate difficult feelings, children feel enabled to resolve their problems.

ELG07: Managing feelings and behaviour – this helps children to adjust their behaviour to different situations and relationships, and cope better with change.

ELG17: Being imaginative – play helps children build better relationships with their peers and the adults responsible for them.

Baby dolls

To encourage recovery of nurture and
stages of development, which some
children miss due to trauma and neglect,
invite them to play with baby dolls and to
give the dolls the care they (the children)
would like for themselves.

Provide dolls, bath, baby lotion, warm
water, towels, fleecy blankets, dolls
clothes, nappies, dolly plates, bottles, cups, dishes, pretend food items, spoons, etc.
A small wheelie case is useful. Follow the child's lead. If the child treats the 'baby' in
an abusive way (hitting and scolding), reflect on how this makes you feel and ask what
the baby did wrong. Explain, *'Babies can't ever be bad.'* Invite the child to create a story
about looking after babies. This could involve a (pretend) trip to a park, shops, or
doctor. Allow the child to lead the play and to allot the roles required. It could include
making telephone calls (see Chapter 5). Through expressing concern for the 'baby'
(doll), you, the adult, will convey that children are entitled to being treated well and
are deserving of your genuine interest and concern.

EARLY LEARNING GOALS

ELG05: Health and self-care – from understanding babies' needs, children learn
about the importance of keeping healthy and safe.

ELG07: Managing feelings and behaviour – children gain confidence to talk about how
babies show feelings; they learn to think about the implications for their own and
others' behaviour, and its consequences.

ELG08: Making relationships – this is enabled from gaining security.

Emotion stones

Emotion stones are pebble-sized stones,
which are painted or engraved with facial
expressions of the common emotions.
They are useful for inviting the children to
talk about their feelings. The child can sit
with a stone in their hands. The idea is to
give them something to hold on to while

talking about their memories of experiences played out that bring up emotions that can sometimes be quite overwhelming..

ELG06: Self-confidence and self-awareness – from talking about their difficult feelings, children feel validated and gain self-confidence.

ELG07: Managing feelings and behaviour – talking about feelings helps children gain self-control and the ability to think about others.

Scripts and strategies

Sense of self

Children who have a negative sense of their identity are likely to be pre-occupied or so easily overwhelmed by feelings of inadequacy that they struggle to see the wider picture. Such a child may want to be the 'boss' all the time and complain, *'They won't play with me, I have no friends'*. If another child tries to take over, the child may assume, *'She hates me'*.

Tell the child that you have lots of time to listen and you want to know what her friends said that upset her so much. Explain that everyone likes being in charge some of the time, and this means taking turns and sharing. Encourage the child to practice fictional friendship situations in play. Regard 'helpless' requests such as, *'You do it for me!'* as a disguised form of power. Help the child to complete tasks by breaking down each step into smaller steps. Assure her that you have plenty of time to do it with her. At mealtimes, demonstrate how to share things around.

Teaching empathy

When a child focuses on things (food or material objects) more than people it could indicate that in her experience, inanimate objects are more constant and dependable for comfort than people. Perhaps her attachment figures have slipped in and out of her life unpredictably, hence proved unreliable. If in the course of play, the child doesn't react to the 'baby' (doll) being hurt and shows only hurt for herself, she may not have developed empathy for other people.

Through stories and dramatic play, we can build the child's social skills for making and sustaining friendships by helping them learn to recognise social signals and practice these skills in fictional scenes then apply them in real life.

Enabling focus

When a child flits constantly from one activity to another, try following him and notice what appeals to him. If he hides, initiate a game of 'hide and seek'. If he likes sorting toys, provide containers and offer to pass things to him. Build on the interests he shows by playing alongside him to keep him engaged.

Early years practitioners can create a possible lines of development or PLOD chart which lists areas of learning. The aim **is** to help the child move to the next step in learning, however small it is. Start by placing the child's interest at the centre of the chart. Moving outwards, make a list of activities the child enjoys. Ask open-ended questions and suggest ideas based on the child's own cues. If the child is not giving any cues, use your imagination.

The child's concentration on a task will improve if you give him objects to mess about with such as a roll of masking tape, and allow him to tape pieces of furniture together. Alternatively, you could give him a ball of knitting yarn, which he can take up and downstairs, weaving patterns as he goes round the staircase and furniture.

Affirmation

Children need to communicate their feelings in order to be able to cope with them. We can't discourage negative feelings out of existence. To deny or repress feelings is only likely to lead to the child's problems becoming worse.

Instead, acknowledge his angry feelings. *'Something is making you feel really cross, isn't it? That's so hard for you!'* To protect the walls and furniture from getting battered in aggressive play, such as crashing of toy cars, place pillows and cushions along the wall and foot of the sofa. If in pretend play the child 'shoots' you, shoot back, saying *'I got you too!'* Ask, *'Who's on your side? Whose soldiers are faster and stronger?'* Allowing the child's team to win will help him master his aggressive feelings in the safe context of play.

Modelling

Children depend on parents to provide love, comfort and pleasure to balance life's frustrations. This can be achieved through giving the child a hug, making eye contact as you talk to her, smiling and comforting her when she wants this, as well as playing with her. During the second year of life, children begin to resolve their aggressive and loving feelings at a feeling and behavioural level. But this does not yet happen on a conceptual level, so they might bite a doll, then, later on in the day, hug it. Acknowledge the feelings they display and comfort anxious children. This will help them to accept limits and move on.

Expanding the play

When play becomes too repetitive it is hard not to get a bit bored. Try making suggestions to develop the play, such as:

Let's have more guests to the 'party'!
Shall we bring the wounded 'soldiers' to hospital?
I reckon these racing cars could do with more 'pit stops'!
Perhaps these cars that have run out of fuel and need mending could do with more mechanics after all this racing! What do you think?

Ask what the characters in the play are saying to each other. This will encourage the child to put his thoughts and feelings into words.

9 Transition

Introduction

Transition is an inevitable part of life and moving on to another stage. It is generally healthy and welcomed. However as O'Connor (2018) explains, where insecure children with poor self-esteem are concerned, transitions involving care and education can cause difficulties. Struik (2019: 154) refers to the 'relay stick of attachment' that gets passed on when the child is moved to new caregivers, until repeated changes of care cause his traumatic memories of abandonment to become too painful for him to keep hold of this relay stick. A risk is that after being moved several times, traumatised children will develop a superficial attachment to their caregivers but remain loyal to their birth parents.

The more placements and changes of caregiver that children have the more they come to expect to be rejected and moved on. In any case, young children in pre-school often need help to adapt to changes, especially if they have already had several changes of caregiving. The child may struggle to cope with even small changes such as a change of room or of the person helping them in nursery – in fact, with anything unfamiliar to him or her.

Magical thinking

Children under five typically use 'magical thinking' (Fraiberg, 2006) (see Glossary). They misinterpret realities and convince themselves that they make things happen simply by wishing it (such as believing the people on TV are speaking directly to them). Accordingly, when families are in difficulty, children are likely to believe they are the cause of the problem and therefore to blame for their fate. The child whose mother is mentally ill might assume that her illness was caused by his 'bad' behaviour. It is important to reassure him that he did nothing to make his mum ill – this did not happen because of him.

Repression and the fear of rejection

Children who have been subjected to traumatic neglect and abuse often experience additional changes in care as further rejection. This can leave them feeling unwanted, inadequate and unable to believe that anyone cares about them. If the (birth) parent is sick or mentally unwell the child may have repressed his own needs to avoid upsetting his parent. Repressed feelings – like a pressure cooker – tend to explode eventually. Even so, we know from enquiries into the deaths of children such as Victoria Climbié (Laming, 2003), Peter Connolly (Laming, 2009), and Daniel Pelka (Rogers, 2013) that many abused children cease to signal their needs due to their fear of reprisal. Indeed, these enquiries found the children masked their terror by smiling as though they felt joyful. New caregivers may not know when a defended child is hurting, hungry, scared, in discomfort or has simply not understood them.

We have all come to know from the experience of lockdown and social isolation the frustration and anxiety emanating from not knowing when it will end. Imagine, then, the anxiety for young children who, after several moves and changes of care, are feeling in a perpetual intense state of anxiety from not knowing what is going to happen to them or when to expect the next change to their living situation. How hard must it be to form a trusting relationship with a caregiver when previously you have only ever been let down and received no clear understanding as to the reason for it?

Traumatised children, although hypervigilant (see Glossary), sometimes 'cut out' the real world and fail to hear what is being said to them. Others chatter incessantly and ask questions but do not listen to the answers. If the adult's attention wanders, the abused child panics. Knowing he can't be 'good' all the time, on being told 'No' he is easily overwhelmed by his anger, frustration, anxiety and sadness – feelings which reinforce his sense of abandonment.

The important message here is that young children who are undergoing changes in their care and education need to be prepared for these changes.

Preparation for transition

To help children accommodate to impending changes in their home situation or education, preparation needs to be carried out in a mode geared to their age and stage of development, using the kind of images and language they will understand. Blackmore et al (2020) found visual and audio materials, such as photographs and video recordings shared by the previous carers, useful for enabling even very young children to accommodate to their adoptive placement. Many early years practitioners use such materials to help children cope in pre-school. Hashmi et al (2020) also advocate doll play for developing social skills and empathy. In research of children aged 4 to 8 years, they found doll play to exercise the parts of the brain employed in social processing and behaviours. Doll play encourages children to build their own imaginary worlds and to think about how other people might interact with each other. For children who have undergone significant and challenging changes in their life, this is especially pertinent to finding a way to explore their experience of life. Children need to know their life history. Caregivers can make a life storybook with them and encourage them to draw pictures of the people they love and live with now, accompanied by photos to clarify the verbal explanations. This will help the children to make sense of what has happened to them. Children can also be engaged in creating rituals, which, combined with creative imaginative play, helps them prepare for transitions and build trusting relationships.

Key points

- It is important to find out the child's interests and focus on these to help her to express herself creatively.

- Play is a natural way for children to explore experience and feelings.

- It is just as important to allow children to express their negative feelings as their positive ones.

Case examples
Danny, aged 4
Danny was living with family friends at the request of his mother. She suffered from bouts of schizophrenia and spent frequent episodes in a psychiatric hospital. Danny had no visual memory of her. After three years in foster care, he assumed that his foster carer was his mummy and wanted to return to her. He didn't understand why he'd been moved to these family friends he had not seen since his infancy. His speech was poor and these parents had to repeat instructions many times before they could get him to comply. Finding Danny to be hyperactive, over-excitable and disruptive, they disapproved of his addiction to movies, videos and online games, and tried to wean him off videos of Ben 10. It hadn't occurred to them that joining him in playing out stories about this character could help them make an emotional connection with Danny and they were most impressed when it soon did so.

Danny loved the cartoon character Ben 10 and connected strongly to a story about this character's adventures. In this story, Ben 10 leaves his home and loses his Omnitrix watch, his most valued possession. Ben 10 felt that he had lost all his power and was horribly confused at being taken to live in a new family.

Danny asked for the story to be reread several times. As his new mother joined in the play that followed, she soon noticed the positive impact this had on their relationship, now that Danny saw her as a playmate as well as a caregiver.

A life map illustrating the houses Danny had lived in served to explain the reasons for the big changes in his life. The map featured Danny's current home, his foster home, his birth parents' homes, nursery, Court, the hospital where he was born, and the hospital treating his mother. Danny chose toy figures to represent the people in his life. These were used to enact scenes in which his moves were replayed. He progressed to creating stories about Spiderman, whose alter ego Peter Parker is adopted by relatives. Danny noticed that Spiderman used his experience to help other people. This story-themed 'hero play' helped Danny to accept his situation and feel ready to attach more securely to his new family. His problematic behaviours abated substantially.

Nina, aged 4

Nina had been terrorised on witnessing her parents' domestic disputes, drug addiction and alcoholism. Her birth mother, having been sexually abused in childhood, was self-harming and diagnosed to have a borderline personality disorder. Nina's father was adopted as a child but sent back to foster care in his teens. As a young adult he stole weapons and threatened social workers. Nina saw him smash up her toys and her mother's phone. She watched as her mother destroyed his car in retaliation. As the row escalated, Nina's Daddy hurled a lawnmower through a window, causing the flying glass to cut her face. Nina arrived in foster care with a chesty cough and bags of wet clothes stinking of cigarettes. Withdrawn and expressionless, she was observed pressing her hands into her eyes to stop the flood of tears.

In nursery, Nina browsed through the toys desultorily, unsure of what to do until she alighted on some tiny dolls clipped together. She danced round with them in the manner of an infant and joined in singing, *'Ring a Ring a Roses'*. Then, seeing paper and crayons, Nina drew three faces – one with a smile, one had the mouth in a straight line and the third, a frown. Her EYP teacher wondered if any of these faces was hers. Nina pointed to the frowning one. Reflecting on these feelings, the teacher drew three houses – the family home where Nina's mummy lived, her daddy's current home, and the foster home. Nina asked her to draw a heart for all these people. The teacher drew a heart next to each house, with a *'river of happy, sad and lonely feelings'* (Corrigan and Moore, 2011) between them. Nina studied it thoughtfully and told her that Mummy 'smelled funny' and 'wound Daddy up'. She felt sad when they fought and upset when they hit her. The teacher wondered which house she wanted to live in. Nina pointed to the foster home. Over the next few weeks, they drew more hearts and cut out chains of paper hearts that Nina stuck together to make a book of hearts. Expressing her feelings in play helped Nina process her fears and build a secure attachment to her teacher and foster carer.

Activities

Dolls and dolls houses

Doll play is a way for young children to explore their impending as well as previous experience of transitions. Ideally have two doll's houses but if you don't have them, use cardboard boxes, e.g. shoeboxes, or areas can be set out with doll's house furniture,  to represent the child's new 'school' or new 'home'. Invite the child or children to rehearse a forthcoming move but let them lead the play. To explore their fears and expectations, you might wonder aloud.

Will the character in the story:

- make a new friend?

- know where to hang their coat?

- know to ask where the toilet is?

- worry about what their new teachers might be like?

- want to know what size of bed they will have?

- worry who they will be sharing a bedroom with?

- be curious about what food they will be given?

- worry about what will happen if they don't eat the food?

- worry about what will happen if they wet the bed?

- worry about if they do something naughty – draw on walls, etc.?

EARLY LEARNING GOALS

ELG03: Speaking – this activity enables children to talk about their past and events they expect to happen, and develop narratives by connecting ideas.

ELG06: Self-confidence and self-awareness – to say when they need help.

ELG08: Making relationships – the child will learn to show sensitivity to others' needs and feelings, and form better relationships.

ELG14: The world – children will talk about the features of their own immediate environment and how they vary.

ELG17: Role-play and story making enables exploring of thoughts and ideas.

Road of feelings

Draw a simple map of the neighbourhood where the child is living, and encourage her to practice an impending move to her new home or school. Use toy people and cars to enact the move. Have a puppet talk about feelings aroused for the child (see Chapter. 5). Say, *'Here we have the road of happy, sad and lonely feelings'* and encourage the child to explore her feelings about what has happened to her. Puppets are very useful for talk about feelings.

EARLY LEARNING GOALS

ELG01: Listening and attention – this activity develops children's ability to listen, pay attention, talk about their feelings, and improve their language.

ELG02: Understanding – the map helps children to make sense of their past.

ELG12: Shape, space and measures – drawing the maps enables children to draw and describe shapes, space and measures.

Map of the future

The child who is due to move to a new family can be invited to draw a map of her ideal home and give it a name, such as 'the chocolate house'. The child can add her school

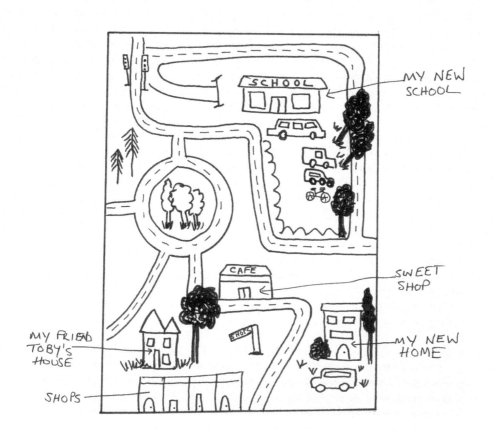

and places such as a dance school, park, pizza restaurant, playground, an animal sanctuary. This map will encourage the child to think about her hopes, ambitions and wishes for the future. Using toy people, play out scenes of how she sees her future.

ELG01: Listening and attention – this activity develops children's ability to listen, pay attention, talk about their feelings, and improve their language.

ELG12: Shape, space and measures – drawing the maps enables children to draw and describe shapes, space and measures.

ELG13: People and communities – the children will talk about past and current events in their lives and in the lives of their family members.

ELG14: The world – children explore varying features of their environment.

ELG16: Exploring and using media and materials – in the course of drawing these maps children learn about using media and materials in original ways, through which they represent their own thoughts, feelings and ideas.

Hero story of adversity

To encourage children to find ways of coping with their worries, find a story with a character such as Elsa (from the film *Frozen*) or some other superhero that the child is likely to connect with. Create a story about this character having to deal with various testing situations but surviving. Stories in the Appendices provide models to draw from. Read the story *A Brave Kitten Called Jingle* (Appendix 5, Story 3) or use it as a model for creating your own story. The story you create might be about a young bird in need of a safe nest or a delicate flower that has to be moved to a new garden with better soil. Or it could be about a prince or princess whose royal parents squabble; or a young animal separated from its parent. Most young children relate well to stories in which the hero is, for example, a young elephant, lion, bird, cat, dog or dinosaur (see Moore 2012, 2014).

Start the story by having the mother express delight in her baby. Let's say the daddy abandons her. Being lonely, the mother (creature) drinks 'dandelion juice' (like drugs) that leaves her too sick to look after her babies. The hungry youngsters have to search for food in order to survive. They might fall into slimy ditches, get stung and injured but have to wait ages to be rescued. Reflect on how strange it feels to live with different species. After telling the story invite the child to re-enact it using toys, dolls or puppets.

As you talk about the feelings arising in the story, children invariably make connections to their own experience. Check they understand the words you are using. Try to keep to the context of the story to ensure the child's privacy. For example, in relation to a story about an abandoned puppy you might remark on how scary or horrible it was for the puppy and how very brave he has been. It is best to avoid direct comparisons to the children, which could shame or embarrass them. If the child says, 'That's my story!' look amazed and remark on how brave he or she is.

EARLY LEARNING GOALS

ELG01: Listening and attention – listening to stories enables children to anticipate key events and demonstrate understanding in talking about them.

ELG06: Self-confidence and self-awareness – children explore their ideas, choose resources and say when they do or don't need help.

ELG09: Reading – will also help children to identify with the hero's fortitude.

ELG14: The world – the child makes observations that help her to notice changes and explain why certain things occur.

ELG17: Being imaginative – this activity will stimulate imagination and encourage children to use their learning in original ways, such as through role-play.

Dramatic play of transition

Dramatic play can be a wonderful way for children to rehearse forthcoming transitions and practice ways of coping via acting a fictional role. Provide a variety of fabrics (ideally some exotic, sparkly ones). Spread lengths of cloth around. This will show the child how easily the room is transformed into, say, a palace, or a landscape of a beach, forest, mountains, or volcano. Alternatively, the setting could be a planet in outer space, a circus or safari park, and so on. Pieces

of material can be turned into cloaks or costumes for magic dragons and fairy godmothers. Useful props include: play money, bags, purses, 'Aladdin's magic lamp', small swords (see Chapter 3 for guidance), scarves, headwear, helmets, wigs, etc.

Invite the child to develop a story about a character whose life is about to change. Start with a magic carpet ride. Let the child decide where to land.

The point of transforming the space is that creating change in the fictional context conveys that such desired change can also happen in real life.

EARLY LEARNING GOALS

ELG03: Speaking – this mode of play enables children to explore their creativity and make sense of their feelings and experiences.

ELG04: Moving and handling – this is an opportunity to gain confidence from moving in a range of ways, safely negotiating the space.

ELG06: Self-confidence and self-awareness – children explore their ideas, choose resources and say when they do or don't need help.

ELG08: Making relationships – in dramatic play, children learn to play cooperatively and take account of other's ideas, sensitivity to needs and feelings.

ELG13: People and communities – children learn similarities and differences among families, communities and traditions.

ELG16: Exploring and using media and materials – children develop their own narratives from connecting ideas and events.

ELG17: Being imaginative – it is an opportunity for sharing ideas, thoughts and feelings via music, movement, dance and play.

Story bags

A variety of materials placed in a bag can be used to encourage children in storytelling.

Step 1 – Preparation:

Fill a bag with diverse items of varying texture and purpose, such as a small mirror, cotton wool, a leaf, conker, shell,

wooden spoon, button, small ball of yarn, and so on. It is a good idea to also have some paper, crayons, and collage materials available.

Step 2 – Involve the child:

Encourage the child to select six items for telling a story about a journey on which each of these items will feature and represent a part of the story.

Step 3 – Structure:

Invite the child think of (1) a hero for their story; (2) someone (or something) to help the hero; (3) where the hero will go on his journey; (4) something that will cause a problem; (5) a solution, and (6) how it all turns out in the end.

Step 4 – Illustrating the story:

Give the children a piece of paper and invite them to use collage materials: sequins, pipe cleaners, ribbon, glue, glitter, etc. Older children can make six pictures – one picture for each part of their story (as in step 3). Younger children could depict an aspect of a story of their own choosing.

EARLY LEARNING GOALS

ELG13: People and communities – this activity is especially effective for enabling children's understanding of their physical world and community.

ELG14: The world – this activity gives children the opportunity to explore, and find out about people and their environment.

ELG16: Exploring and using media and materials – children can use a wide range of media and materials, tools and techniques.

ELG17: Being imaginative – story bags and storytelling stimulate imagination.

Clay for rebuilding

Air-drying modelling clay starts off as wet and sticky then gradually dries and hardens with exposure to the air. From discovering that clay changes form, children learn subconsciously that things change and that the same principle can apply to relationships, so as we get to know and trust people, we too can adapt. Invite the child to model various shapes and create a story about them. See Chapter 2 for more ideas on making clay people. A useful story to share is *Milo and the Magical Stones*, by Marcus Pfeifer (1997). In this story, mice discover shiny golden stones in a cave under their mountain home. There are two outcomes, positive and negative. In the negative ending, the failure of greedy mice to replace the stones causes the mountain to collapse. But in the positive outcome, the mice replace the stones they borrowed so the mountain remains intact and the mice go on to enjoy daily celebrations of storytelling.

After hearing the story, invite the children to use modelling clay or play dough to construct the mice, mountain and magic stones. Suggest the mice go on a journey to collect treasures. Encourage the child to decorate clay 'stones' with leaves, seeds and patterns. Talk about how important it is to have treasures. If the child is moving to a new home or school, they may need to decide what to take and leave beforehand. The child might choose to hide certain items or people in the (clay or play dough) mountain. Explore the motive for hiding things. Does the child want to keep the hidden objects or people safe, or could she be expressing the fear of never being found? Encourage the child to develop her story and talk about the arising feelings.

EARLY LEARNING GOALS

ELG02: Understanding – this activity enables children to improve their understanding as they make connections between actions, ideas and events.

ELG04: Moving and handling – play with clay facilitates coordination by using fine motor skills in handling equipment and tools and trying out techniques

ELG06: Self-confidence and self-awareness – increase with competence.

ELG08: Making relationships – children learn to show sensitivity and to respect similarities and differences between themselves and others.

ELG16: Exploring and using media and materials – this activity encourages creativity and imagination using a variety of tools.

Baking biscuits

Mixing, cutting (with shape cutters), and baking biscuits and buns is a nurturing activity that will encourage young children to feel more ready to attach to their caregiving parents. The smell of baking is particularly inviting. Once cooled, the biscuits can be iced and decorated. Invite the children to make designs on iced biscuits to give to someone else and exchange the biscuit for one the other person designs for them.

Ingredients for the biscuits

- 100g unsalted butter at room temperature
- 100g caster sugar
- 1 medium free-range egg, beaten
- 1 teaspoon vanilla extract
- 275g plain flour

For icing and decorating

- 400g icing sugar
- 3–4 tablespoons lemon juice/water
- 2–3 drops of food colouring (optional)
- Decorations, tubes for writing, letters, shapes

Method

Preheat oven to 190C/375F/Gas 5. Line baking tray with greaseproof paper.

1. Cream the butter and sugar together in a bowl until combined.
2. Add the egg and vanilla extract, a little at a time, and beat until combined.
3. Stir in the flour until the mixture comes together as a dough.
4. Roll the dough out on a lightly floured worktop to a thickness of 1cm.
5. Cut biscuit shapes out of the dough and place on baking tray.
6. Bake for 6–10 minutes, until pale golden brown. Remove from oven and set aside to harden for five minutes then cool on wire rack.
7. For the icing, sift icing sugar in a bowl and stir in enough lemon juice to make a smooth mixture that is not too runny and add a few drops of colouring if required.

Developing Secure Attachment

ELG06: Self-confidence and self-awareness – enhances self-esteem. The baking smells make the experience of it all the more nurturing and enjoyable.

ELG12: Shape, space and measures – this activity invites pattern making.

Scripts and strategies

Building sense of security

For a frightened child who is starting nursery, the strangeness of the noise, activity levels and new people can feel overwhelming. It is best for the parent to remain in the classroom with the child initially, for 15 to 20 minutes or for however long it takes. This avoids a power struggle at the door and shows the child that it is a safe place for her to be. Gradually the teacher will become the secure person to whom she attaches in the educational setting. The child might be encouraged to play with one or two others. Otherwise, you can sit with her in a quiet corner and see if she will play out a scene with a few toy animals or dolls, in which these characters leave each other and later reunite.

Role-play changes

To practice ways of managing transitions, encourage the child to take the role of, say, parent, teacher or doctor in a fictional (story) context. In this way the child learns about other people's points of view and practices ways of dealing with changes. Stories will often develop from creative play. Chat with the story 'characters' and invite the child to think of magical transformations.

Routines

Create new routines, such as playing games on the way to and from nursery or school. Invent a special greeting to convey how important the child is to you. Create new rituals, e.g. after school, when the child has dropped his coat on the floor, try singing, *'This is where the coats hang up, coats hang up, coats hang up, this is where the coats hang up and this is where we do it'*. Joining in singing these songs will enable the child's sense of belonging.

Photos

To ease school transition for anxious children, have photos of the teacher, the school entrance and the child's classroom. Where looked after and adopted children are concerned, early years practitioners are advised to ask the caregiving parent, who is collecting the child, to provide photos that the EYPs can show the child to reassure her of who she is going home with.

Calendars

Pictorial calendars illustrate what will happen on which days and can be used to help children cope better with moving to a new family, nursery or school. See the illustrated photo board and calendar in Chapter 4 for ideas.

Show she is in your mind

Sometimes parents have to leave a child, who wants their attention, to attend to the child's sibling. This may raise the anxious child's sense that he is no longer important. Similarly, in school or nursery, the practitioner will sometimes have to leave the anxious child (and attend to someone else). To reassure the child who feels abandoned, give her a task or an item to look after. Mention her name so that she knows you are thinking about her. Give her jobs that will enhance her status such as feeding the class pet. Involve her in projects that can use her talents and cooperation. If the child is struggling with even a very small thing, show your deep interest and promise her that together you will try to find a way round this problem. See strategies in Chapter 4 for more ideas.

Peer support

Early years practitioners could talk with the rest of the group about how the children can support each other in the class and play area. They could find the lonely child a sensitive 'buddy' to help the child feel included in activities. Assess whether the child needs and responds better to one-on-one attention or to a small group to help her or him develop friendship skills.

Home–school book

Communicate with caregivers via a home–school book and/or email/text message. Early years practitioners should avoid blaming and shaming over-stressed and anxious parents and caregivers.

10 Identity

Introduction

Children depend on their parents to model how to interact, adjust to social situations and care about other people. Unfortunately, the poor interaction of some parents with their children forms a 'cycle of discord' (Patterson, 2002). The legacy of neglect and abuse leaves many of the most vulnerable children in public care with a negative sense of their identity, which frequently replicates that of their birth parents. They need help to build a more positive sense of self, which evolves from gaining a feeling of belonging. Extensive literature and government guidance emphasises that building children's sense of identity is one of the most important aspects in achieving positive outcomes, particularly for children in care and who are adopted. This chapter illustrates how the philosophy, theory and practice of this book can be applied to older traumatised children, who benefit as much as younger ones from activities enabling recovery of nurture and missed stages of development.

Contexts of identity

Emotional development takes place in the cultural context in which children are developing their identity. Identity means both sameness (shared physical and personality characteristics) and individuality (the things that mark us out as unique and different to everyone else). Pre-school children are just starting to find out which personalities and talents they already have and might start to develop, such as the tendency to be generous or mean, to be a risk taker or avoid risk, to be clever or slow, lazy or active, and so on. Identity is to do with how you think and feel about yourself, what you believe in, your hopes, dreams, ambitions, commitments to particular ways of life. It is also about how others define you. Influences include culture, community, social class, religion, race/ethnicity/heritage, ability/disability, gender and sexual identity.

In some cultures parents raise children to be independent at an earlier age, whilst in others, children are raised to be dependent on the family group. This makes it especially important to take cultural factors into account before making critical judgements about how a parent is raising their child.

Culture and ethnicity

The cultural dimension to identity is particularly significant for children living in a family in which the parents' ethnicity and physical appearance is patently different to theirs. The controversial practice of transracial adoption, most often of placing ethnic minority children with white parents, is criticised because of the potential risk of inhibiting the children's ethnic identity development (Padilla et al, 2010). Adoptive parents may try to deny the relevance of the child's colour in a desire to be inclusive but children will always see colour and notice who is similar and who is different. It is important to talk to children about issues of race and help them develop a positive identity. Hughes (2020), in cooperation with a foster carer, argues for same race placements and shows how the acculturation process can be effectively achieved for a young child. While it is important to honour the child's birth culture, it is important to explore how they feel about it, as not all children automatically identify with their birth culture.

Substance dependency

The demands of parenting, particularly for disadvantaged families coping with other stress-inducing factors, can be intense and challenging. Parents use a range of strategies to cope with stress. When the strategies involve drinking alcohol, taking illegal drugs, or smoking, for example, they help to alleviate the parents' stress in the short term but they can also leave them less emotionally available and less protective of their children (or the children in their care) in the long run. The children learn that chemicals are to be relied on rather more than their own inner resources. The culture internalised is one of dependence that may affect their sense of identity and how they go on to function as individuals. A significant proportion of affected children have to be removed to safer care.

Coping with change

In the new environment, young children inevitably become increasingly receptive to the specific rules of behaviour they are being taught. Dozier et al (2002) described the confusion for children when they are moved back and forth between foster care and the birth family, each living by an entirely different set of rules. Accommodating to these changes can feel like having to learn a new language each time. Multiple moves require children to keep adjusting, which makes it very difficult for them to retain a sense of identity built on belonging. Lindsey and Kenrick (2019) remind us that the very concept of what a mother or father, sister or brother is supposed to be can be confusing for children who have had changes of care and abuse from a caregiver.

Negative identity

Jumbo had a baby dressed in green
Wrapped it up in paper and sent it to the Queen.
The Queen did not like it because it was too fat.
She cut it up in pieces and gave it to the cat.
The cat did not like it because it was too thin.
She cut it up in pieces and gave it to the King.
The King did not like it because it was too slow.
Threw it out the window and gave it to the crow.

(Bowlby, 1973: 18)

The poem above illustrates the fragility of identity for a child who is feeling rejected, deserted and unloved. Abuse, especially when combined with lots of changes of care, inevitably sets children back. It causes them to develop a negative sense of identity – a belief that whatever happened to cause the rejection was their fault. The child reasons that he must be 'bad' so deserves rejection and abandonment, which he comes to expect the more it happens. As with any traumatic reminder, children easily revert emotionally to the age at which the first upsetting separation from their parent occurred. In the hyper-arousal of trauma, they do not have the words to explain their feelings and behaviour. The stress on new caregivers can lead to 'secondary trauma' (Figley, 1995) and to the family requiring specialist help from a therapist who understands the child's background and the strain they are all under.

Key points

- Empathy and play are key to change.

- Understanding their life story helps reduce children's tendency to self-blame.

- In play, fictional scenarios permit naughtiness not allowed in real life. This encourages exploration of the full range of feelings in a safe context.

- Play enables us to challenge children's negative self-beliefs.

Case examples
Ivan, aged 7

Ivan, the youngest of four children in his birth family, was taken into foster care at five years of age, having suffered chronic neglect and hunger. He had also witnessed his parents' violence, drug taking and inappropriate sexual boundaries. Ivan had four foster placements before he was placed for adoption at the age of seven. He was unable to settle in school, where the staff felt threatened by his behaviour. For Ivan, the experience of being in the classroom felt far too frightening to face. Within a few months of being placed in his adoptive family, the demise of his birth mother added to his distress and anxiety. Life story therapy was sought to help Ivan reconcile to being adopted.

HOW GUIDED PLAY THERAPY HELPED

Ivan could not explain how he came to live in his adoptive family but remarked that he really missed his siblings. Using a life map of the houses he'd lived in and toy figures to represent the people (see Chapter 8), scenes from his life story were enacted, beginning with his birth parents' childhoods to illustrate the stress they had grown up with. His adoptive parent and therapist remarked on Ivan inheriting his birth dad's practical skills. Ivan admitted to mixed memories of his birth mother. He knew he loved her even though she had not even taught him how to use the toilet. He recalled wearing nappies until he was five, never cleaning his teeth and being hungry from a diet mainly of sweets. Ivan chose a plant and drew a picture he wished to give his (late) birth mother. He was reassured to be told that he deserved a family, who would give him the best care possible. Ivan seemed to accept the explanation that his birth parents had been unable to do this due to having no example to draw from. After the water game (see Chapter 8), which Ivan greatly enjoyed, he clung to his adoptive mum and, like a toddler, refused to let her out of his sight.

Ivan's play featured soldiers, who admitted to being terrified of violence, yet were fighting in sandstorms that obliterated their vision. Initially there was a sense of despair and hopelessness as dinosaurs relentlessly threatened to kill Captain America (Ivan's hero). In response to a suggestion that Captain America needed help from his own kind, Ivan brought in more superheroes but the violence did not abate. His assumption was that everyone would die. The therapist remarked that luckily, as a race, we humans have survived so far. Ivan had his 'dinosaurs' produce babies and declared they were taught well. He went on to create montages of his current life, playing football, running on the beach, Dad sprinting, Ivan at an athletics club, eating his first curry, playing on climbing frames, singing in the Christmas play, baking, welding, forklift with Dad, bowling with grandparents, gardening, dressing up and messy play.

A few days later Ivan was brooding, expecting that as he had moved so many times, his adoptive parents would reject him before much longer. Distressed, he placed his knife and fork on the floor to eat there and eventually explained, *'I can't live anywhere. My life will be too hard and I can't get through it. I will be in jail as I won't be able to live a life.'* His adoptive parents hugged him and thanked him for telling them his worries. They reassured him that life with them would mean having fun, friends and learning new things as well as doing boring things. Ivan asked how to be a good person and they promised to guide him as best they could. Mum drew a life path on a long strip of paper to show the time he had spent in each home before (and since) living with her. The first section was of Ivan's life in his birth family (five years). The next was divided into five sections – the first four for the period he was in foster care. The remaining section was for the time in his adoptive family. The rest of the strip, of much greater length, showed how much of his life (up to 21 years) was still ahead. Ivan coloured it in, now feeling calm and hugely reassured.

Ivan enjoyed playing 'Animal Olympics' (Chapter 6) with puppets. He ran outside and jumped around. Ivan relished messy play, in which (cold cooked) spaghetti became 'scenery' for his dinosaurs. In one story he described the main character as *'8 years old. He had always been bad, he wasn't able to be good'*. The therapist speculated that this young dinosaur had not been looked after when he was little. Lost, he and his brother search for each other. On reuniting, one blames the other (revealing Ivan's sense of loss for which he blamed himself). Eventually the 'bad' brother transforms into a strong hero and makes friends. Ivan was daring to hope that he too, might transform.

Gradually Ivan was able to extend his time in the classroom so that in the following term he was able to last all day. Ivan could now coherently explain and describe things he was learning about, and amuse himself for half an hour, having moved beyond the immature stage he had been stuck in. He became more securely attached to his nurturing adoptive parents, who learned to respond to the age he was displaying at any one moment.

Mia, aged 8

Mia, of Indian and white English heritage, was a few days old when taken to foster care. She was subsequently placed for adoption with a white mother and Indian father of matching ethnicity. Mia's birth mother had learning difficulties and had been unable to protect her children from partners, who were drug-addicted and known sex offenders. At age 8, Mia was referred for life story therapy due to her separation anxiety and frequent tantrums. She was distractible in school and finding it difficult to explain to her peers why she was adopted. Mia had begun asking for more detail about her life story and origins.

HOW LIFE STORY THERAPY HELPED

Entranced to see her life map (see Chapter 8), Mia drew her school and family and went on to create a story about the disposal of evil. Later, at bedtime, she asked what happened to her birth mum and whether she, Mia, would still be alive had she stayed with her. Reassured that she would probably be alive but perhaps not very happy, and that she now has parents who can look after her properly, Mia said, *'I'm glad I'm with you guys!'* She wondered why a safe adoptive family had not been found for her birth mum as a child. Mia's adoptive mum explained that social workers don't always know about children but had been alerted by her sister's plight. Mia remarked that this had 'saved' her.

In the water game (Chapter 8), Mia found it painful to hear about her birth parents' difficulties. The therapist explained that lots of problems in their childhood (and since) had prevented them from being able to look after their children because they didn't have the pictures in their minds to show them how to do this. It hadn't been their fault or Mia's fault – it was just bad luck. Mia remarked that she was the only adopted child in her class. Others had asked her about the story of her adoption and she hadn't known how to respond. I remarked that she didn't have to tell them anything but if she wanted to, she could say her birth parents hadn't been well enough to bring her up. Mia enjoyed filling her adoptive 'parent' jugs then letting them fill hers. She described a nightmare in which scary creatures had threatened her. On waking she had gone to her parents. The therapist praised her for knowing what to do and explained dreams as the brain's way of preparing us to deal with our fears. Later Mia asked her adoptive mum why she looks so different to her, worried about the judgements others might be making about her (Mia). Mum advised her that people see them as a family, of which there are many types, and that Mia has a mum who turns up on time and a dad who is great fun to be with.

Mia's stories revealed her concern with looking 'different'. In her play using the sand tray, zoo animals want new clothes so they will look their best for the visitors. Children in care and adopted often experience visits from social workers and associated professionals as a form of 'inspection' and being 'judged' (like zoo animals). In one of Mia's stories, the slaves see the Sultan's evil wife kicking the royal dog so they carry out a plot to poison her. It was Mia's way of unconsciously processing her fear of treachery to which she felt she'd been exposed. Play, like adult dreams, enables children to process their fears subconsciously and achieve power over a sense of oppression.

In another play, a mother and child go to the seaside, where 'They need a passcode to get in. They didn't know the code so they listened to people in the queue.' It expressed Mia's bewilderment about how the adult world works. In this play, it rains, the child gets a lift home but the mother is left behind. Mia's multiple repeated tricking of the 'mother' into believing that she was getting a lift home then getting left behind had the adults in hysterics. Children love to be naughty. Fiction gives permission for this, which helps to make up for the constraints of social convention in real life. Mia may also have been giving her adoptive mum an experience of betrayal she felt from having been removed from her birth mother and sensing a 'difference' to her (white) peers. The story continued with 'mum' flying to America, where she meets her child's identical twin and believes it is actually her daughter. This could have been Mia's exploration of the good/bad self or her musing 'What if there is another me out there? Would she be good or bad, desirable or not?' It is impossible to know what a child is actually thinking and can be intrusive to ask too many questions, which would risk spoiling her trust in the adult as a playmate.

Mia enjoyed nurture play of cooking 'dinner' in a 'sausage machine' that pinged when the meal was ready. She made a (play dough) birthday cake and decorated it with pink hearts and strawberries on chocolate icing. On other occasions Mia had a wonderful time mixing water, flour and shaving foam. She and mum massaged each other's hands. Mia made 'face cream' to make the wearer look 'twenty years younger' and applied it to mum's face.

In doll play the evolving story explored the power that children and parents exercise over each other. It featured a mother, who is patient and hospitable, and her friend, who is variable but learns from her mistakes when tested out. Hence, when her child refuses to come home from a play date, the less secure mum threatens to abandon the child but then relents. The story ends with a sense of optimism and belief in caring for children, indicating Mia's belief in her adoptive parents' capacity and willingness to meet her needs. She told several stories about hurt creatures being mended and looked after.

Developing Secure Attachment

Mia showed determination not to let the past prevent her from making the most of the present and future. She became more comfortable talking about being adopted in a positive light. Mia proved herself to be adept at using her imagination to create stories, which was evidence that she had had plenty of stories read to her and was feeling emotionally well supported by her parents.

Activities
My family as animals

Provide the child with paper and invite her to draw herself and her (current) family as animals. If the child is in a foster or adoptive family, she might also draw her birth family and previous foster family as animals. How she arranges the figures (facing out or facing each other; distant or close, etc.), whether she draws each as the same species or as different ones, can lead to interesting discussions about what the animals have in common, what they share or disagree on, and so on.

It can be enlightening for both child and caregivers to reflect on the shared personality characteristics of these creatures. Some will have mythical qualities, others symbolise motherhood. Ants are tiny creatures yet great at mobilising armies. It is important to avoid making assumptions about the children's projections. For example, the adult on seeing the child's drawing of a sheep might mistakenly infer that it represents someone 'woolly headed' (not very smart) when the child actually chose it to represent sheep as warm and cosy creatures, who (as one child put it) 'always looks after their young'.

EARLY LEARNING GOALS

ELG01: Listening and attention – this activity develops children's ability to listen, pay attention, talk about their feelings, and improve their language.

ELG02: Understanding – talking about their drawings will help children make sense of their past and present relationships and make comparisons.

ELG13: People and communities – the children will talk about past and current events in their lives and in the lives of their family members.

Life story play with costumes and music

It can be huge fun to hold a play of the child's life story. You might first read the story *The Brave Warrior* (Appendix 5, Story 5) to convey how remarkably brave the child was, like the hero, to have survived such hard times. Then invite the child to join in a play about his own life story. The life story play is also a format for exploring the child's real-life experience in a way that has more meaning for the child. Provide a selection of clothing items such as wigs (for judge, for example), hats, scarves, waistcoats and props such as wheelie bags, purses with coins, life size dolls (to represent babies/children), nappies and baby doll equipment. If the child's birth parents were involved in drug addiction

and/or trafficking, it is important to convey that you are not frightened about the past that the child has lived through. Accordingly, it can be useful to have a retractable knife and 'drugs' symbolised by a small bag of salt. A bottle of 'booze' can be represented by a water bottle, while the child can make 'cigarettes' by rolling up small pieces of paper into narrow tubes. The child may remember songs his birth parents liked. Otherwise, songs from the time being enacted can be played on phones to set the scene. It is very important that scenes do not feature actual violence. Instead, convey the 'morning after' by having the social worker call round, for example, after a row between birth parents. Some children love to take part in these plays, others prefer to watch or film (on their phone) scenes taking place between the adult performers.

EARLY LEARNING GOALS

ELG02: Understanding – enacting scenes from their life will help children make sense of their past and present relationships and make comparisons.

ELG13: People and communities – the children will talk about past and current events in their lives and in the lives of their family members.

ELG17: This activity will stimulate imagination and encourage children to use their learning in original ways, such as through role-play.

Safe space

Invite the older child to choose an appealing picture on a postcard, ideally a scene that makes the child feel happy and peaceful. Place the picture in the centre of a piece of A4 paper. Using crayons and/or paint, the child expands the picture to fill the space round it. Then remove the card and invite the child to fill in the gap and say which part of his new picture he likes best. When feeling upset, the child counts to 10 and thinks of this peaceful place.

EARLY LEARNING GOALS

ELG02: Understanding – talking about their drawings will help children make sense of their past and present relationships and make comparisons.

ELG13: People and communities – the children will talk about past and current events in their lives and in the lives of their family members.

'All about me' game

This is a board game for older children, although there are now pre-school versions available. These involve interactive activities such as finger printing and making up your books about yourself. The aim is to encourage children to talk about their feelings and build their sense of identity. You can buy this game equipped with small cards on which are questions 'all about me'. Players take turns to throw the dice and move their piece that number of squares round the board. The player then picks up a card, and answers the question on the card. Caregivers of younger children could make up questions and draw their own board, which the child can illustrate with cut out pictures on a theme such as animals or Disney characters.

ELG01: Listening and attention – listening to stories enables children to anticipate key events and demonstrate understanding in talking about them.

ELG06: Self-confidence and self-awareness – children explore their ideas, choose resources and say when they do or don't need help.

ELG08: Making relationships – children learn to play cooperatively, take account of other's ideas, and be sensitive to needs and feelings.

Photo boards/collages

This is an activity for any age group from 4 to 18 years. Creating photo boards involves covering a board in a montage of photos of the child and her life, to ground her in the family and community she is in at present. Similarly, as well as photos of the child and the people, relatives and friends who she cares about, collages can feature pictures of the activities that she most enjoys.

It can also include pictures of her favourite food, hobbies, interests, toys, etc. This activity can be immensely good for enhancing self-esteem in serving to remind the child of all her positive relationships and the nurturing aspects of her life. Older children can create a separate collage for each phase of their life – for example, their time at nursery, playgroup, and each school they attended. This can lead to making collages of their ambitions, interests, the places they hope to travel to and the careers they aspire to.

ELG02: Understanding – talking about their drawings, photos and pictures will help children to make sense of their past and present relationships and compare the various places or homes where they have lived and been educated.

ELG06: Self-confidence and self-awareness – children explore their ideas, choose their own pictures and say when they do or don't need help.

ELG08: Making relationships – in the course of accepting help children, learn to cooperative, take account of other's ideas and be sensitive to feelings.

Candle ceremonies

These ceremonies can be carried out in several ways. They can help children to say 'goodbye' to the past, address unfinished business and celebrate their enjoyment of a more rewarding lifestyle. Candles (lit by the adult) symbolise each significant person and pet in the child's life (past and present). The lighted candles serve as reminders of warm feelings the child holds for these people. LED candles are useful alternatives where there are restrictions on wax candles. These

ceremonies are an opportunity to reflect on the qualities and skills and abilities of the child, the positive aspect of being given a life, the ability to survive difficulties and to have opportunities to develop talents. The child can address each 'person' represented by a candle, to talk about things he can remember that happened and about how he feels towards the person.

EARLY LEARNING GOALS

ELG02: Understanding – talking about their drawings will help children to make sense of their past and present relationships and compare them.

ELG06: Self-confidence and self-awareness – increases as the child learns about their talents and where they came from.

ELG13: People and communities – the children will talk about past and current events in their lives and in the lives of their family members.

ELG16: Exploring and using media and materials – the children will learn how candles can be safely lit using appropriate tools and techniques.

Card games: UNO, patience, solitaire, pairs, snap

Playing card games is a useful way to engage older children who struggle with play activities that rely more heavily on imagination. Some children are more familiar with card games than with other forms of play. Games such as UNO, patience, solitaire and pairs are easy to follow and unthreatening, not requiring great intellectual capacity. Even pre-school children enjoy games of snap that involve matching picture cards.

The interaction that follows can become a springboard for talking about things that are playing on the child's mind, as well as for building a relationship.

EARLY LEARNING GOALS

ELG02: Understanding – talking about feelings that arise in the game enables children to make sense of their past and present relationships.

ELG03: Speaking – this activity can encourage children to talk about their feelings, events they expect to happen, and to develop narratives by connecting ideas.

ELG06: Self-confidence and self-awareness – children explore their ideas, choose their favourite game and say when they do or don't need help.

ELG08: Making relationships – children learn to play cooperatively, take account of other's ideas, and be sensitive to needs and feelings.

ELG13: People and communities – children often talk about past and current events in their lives and in the lives of their family members while being engrossed in a game that requires relatively little eye contact.

Board games: Snakes and Ladders, Ludo, Monopoly

These board games are fairly undemanding and can often be comfortingly familiar to older children, especially those who spend time in family centres in contact with birth parents. The interaction that follows invites discussion about things that may be bothering the children, while helping to build a relationship with them. The child who is scared of intimacy can share the same settee and accustom himself to the kind of closeness that feels more comfortable to him since it doesn't require eye contact, which for traumatised children can feel quite threatening.

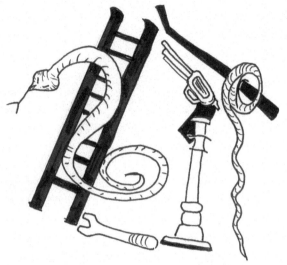

EARLY LEARNING GOALS

ELG02: Understanding – talking about feelings arising in the game enables children to make sense of their past and present relationships.

ELG03: Speaking – this activity can encourage children to talk about their feelings, events they expect to happen, and to develop narratives by connecting ideas.

ELG06: Self-confidence and self-awareness – children explore their ideas, choose their favourite game and say when they do or don't need help.

ELG08: Making relationships – children learn to play cooperatively, take account of other's ideas, and be sensitive to needs and feelings.

Scripts and strategies

Building confidence

Traumatised children can be ultra-sensitive, tricky to engage, and because they lack confidence, inclined to perceive slights where none were intended. One way to engage older children is to place a pack of cards on the table and say, *'I really fancy a game of UNO right now. Would you like to join me?'* If during the game the child gets angry because she is losing, try to notice her frustration at the earliest stage and remark how frustrating it feels not to win. Suggest a compensation for losing too many games such as being given a small snack (such as chopped carrot sticks, a sweet, a few raisins). This conveys to the child that you are on her side whether she wins or loses.

Taking responsibility

Children may lie, cheat, or deny responsibility for their actions regardless of clear evidence of what they've done. Avoid getting into a debate with them about who did what as they are likely to dissociate and convince themselves of their innocence.

Avoid trying to extract any admission of guilt from the child as this will only serve to plunge him into shame, feeling even more unwanted.

Just say what you think must have happened. Let the child know that you know. At a later stage, say you expect that he will make up for it somehow.

Being realistic

Avoid battles you cannot hope to win. As the responsible adult, it is up to you to model how to manage conflict sensibly. This means keeping the heat down while you stand your ground so the child doesn't find that she can control you. If you lose, she loses too. In the heat of the moment she won't realise that, but will just want the satisfaction of being in control (since for her, so much of life feels out of control). Remember she will be acting at a much younger age. Say to her '*I care about you and what you do!*' Acknowledge that you cannot force her to comply but you hope she will so things go better for her. Offer to help her (for example, to clean up her bedroom) as you would a younger child.

Find out the cause

If the child continues to be angry or upset, it may be that he is worrying about something such as an impending contact with someone he is not sure he wants to see, or perhaps a homework task he doesn't understand. It will help if you calmly and uncritically say what you think might really be bothering the child.

If it's the impending contact, you might say something like, '*I'm sorry you're feeling so upset lately. I wonder what is really bothering you? I know you should be meeting your birth mum tomorrow. Are you worried about it? Perhaps you are wondering if she'll have a problem getting there?*'

If you suspect the child worries about failing at school and not understanding homework instructions, you might say, '*I wonder what it is that you're really wound up about. Is it homework? Shall we have a look at it together? Maybe I can help you out?*' Always try to keep your promises.

Engineer positive experiences

It is difficult to live with what may feel like endlessly uncooperative behaviour.

Try making an offer the child can't refuse, so you get the excuse to praise her (for example, offer her favourite meal so you can praise her for eating it). If you have a garden, you could send her on an errand such as collecting (flat) stones that she can later paint. Praise her for whatever she brings in. If she doesn't bring you any stones, say *'Let's make sure you get some more practice at this another time.'* Try to avoid showing disappointment or disapproval, as she will read this and feel down.

Role reversal

A benefit of dramatic play is that it provides the privacy of 'role play' in which the child acts as 'someone else'. It also provides sensory experience, for example, the feeling of movement. You could act out the child's feelings and invite him to respond as you, the adult. As he projects your feelings it can be insightful for both of you.

Appendices

Appendix 1: Early learning goals

Child's Name: ....   Date started:......................

Table A1.1

No:	Early Learning Goal	Date achieved
01	**Communication and Language (Listening and attention)** Listening attentively to a range of situations. Listen to stories and accurately anticipate key events; Respond to what they hear with relevant comments questions, or actions; Give attention to what others say and respond appropriately, while engaged in another activity.	
02	**Communication and Language (Understanding)** Children follow instructions involving ideas or actions. They answer 'how' and 'why' questions about their own experiences and in response to stories or events.	
03	**Communication and Language (Speaking)** Children express themselves self effectively, showing awareness of listeners' needs. They use past, present and future forms accurately when talking about events that have happened or are to happen in the future. They develop their own narratives and explanations by connecting idea or events.	
04	**Physical Development (Moving and handling):** Children show positive control and coordination in large and small movements. They move confidently in a range of ways – safely negotiating space. They handle equipment and tools effectively, including pencils for writing.	

Appendices

No:	Early Learning Goal	Date achieved
05	**Physical Development (Health and self-care)**: Children know the importance for good health of physical exercise, and a healthy diet, and talk about ways to keep healthy and safe. They manage their own basic hygiene and personal needs successfully, including dressing and going to the toilet independently.	
06	**Personal, Social and Emotional Development (Self-confidence and self-awareness)**: Children are confident to try new activities and say why they like some activities more than others. They are confident to speak in a familiar group, will talk about their ideas and will choose the resources they need for their chosen activities. They say when they do or don't need help.	
07	**Personal, Social and Emotional Development (Managing feelings and behaviour)**: Children talk about how they and others show feelings, talk about their own and others' behaviour and its consequences and know that some behaviour is unacceptable. They work as part of a group or class, and understand and follow rules. They adjust their behaviour to different situations, and take changes of routine in their stride.	
08	**Personal, Social and Emotional Development (Making relationships)**: Children play cooperatively, taking turns with others. They take account of another's ideas about how to organise their activity. They show sensitivity to others' needs and feelings, and form positive relationships with adults and other children.	
09	**Literacy (Reading)**: Children read and understand simple sentences. They use phonic knowledge to decode regular words and read them aloud accurately. They also read some common irregular words. They demonstrate understanding when talking with others about what they have read.	

No:	Early Learning Goal	Date achieved
10	**Literacy (Writing)**: Children use their phonic knowledge to write words in ways which match spoken sounds. They also write some irregular common words. They write simple sentences which can be read by themselves and others. Some words are spelt correctly and others are phonetically plausible.	
11	**Mathematics (Numbers)**: Children count reliably with numbers from 1 to 20, place in order and say which number is one more or one less than a given number. Children use quantities and objects. They add and subtract two single digit numbers; they count on or back to find the answer, and solve problems, including doubling, halving and sharing.	
12	**Mathematics (Shape, space and measures)**: Children use everyday language to talk about size, weight, capacity, position, distance, time and money, to compare quantities and objects, and to solve problems. They recognise, create and describe patterns. They explore characteristics of everyday objects and shapes and use mathematical language to describe them.	
13	**Understanding the World (People and communities)**: Children talk about past and present events in their own lives and in the lives of family members. They know that other children don't always enjoy the same things, and are sensitive to this. They know about similarities and differences between themselves and others, and among families, communities and traditions.	
14	**Understanding the World (The world)**: Children know about similarities and differences in relation to places, objects, materials and living things. They talk about the features of their own immediate environment, and how environments vary from one another. They make observations of animals and plants and explain why some things occur, and talk about changes.	

No:	Early Learning Goal	Date achieved
15	**Understanding the World (Technology):** Children recognise that a range of technology is used in places such as homes and schools. They select and use technology for particular purposes.	
16	**Expressive Arts and Design (Exploring and using media and materials):** Children sing songs, make music and dance, and experiment with ways of changing them. They safely use and explore a variety of materials, tools and techniques, experimenting with colour, design, texture, form and function.	
17	**Expressive Arts and Design (Being imaginative)** Children use what they have learnt about media and materials in original ways, thinking about uses and purposes. They represent their own ideas, thoughts and feelings through design and technology, art, music, dance, role-play and stories.	

Appendix 2: Play activities

Cardboard boxes

Can be turned into: TV, car, train, aeroplane, bus, boat, rocket, robot, helmet/mask worn over the head (but cut out eye holes), washing machine, dishwasher, fridge, storage box, cooker, wardrobe, chair, cot/bed, bath, shop, dolls house, den, sledge, hiding place, throwing bean bags into box, or a Post Box for posting letters.

Dressing up

Hats, scarves, helmets, clothes, shoes and wigs.

Lengths of fabric, towels and blankets can be spread to represent 'scenery' – blue for 'sea', red for a 'volcano', yellow for the 'beach', green for 'tree', etc.

Props

Purses, bags, play money, small suitcase on wheels, pram, plastic swords.

Imaginative play settings

For which boxes can be used as:

Palace and Royal Family – king, queen, princess, prince

Doctors and nurses – hospitals, GP surgery

Family home – Mums, Dads and children

The street where you live

Carnivals and festivals

Circus, theatre, cinema

Post Office

Supermarket – goods plus till

Appendices

Adventure assault course

Story making (each box represents a different element in the story)

Train, plane, bus, car

Vets/pet shop/animal hospital

Jungle/zoo/farm

Desert and camels, oasis

Petrol station/garage (mending cars)/car park/car wash

School, playground games (e.g. hopscotch), plus classroom

Chip shop/McDonalds drive thru, pizza parlour/café/restaurant

Outer space – rockets to visit different planets

Castles – fairies, elves, gnomes

Musical boxes – game like musical chairs where you get in a box when the music stops

Holidays – suitcases/tent/caravan

Stables – grooming horses

Survival Camp on a desert island

Mountains and lakes

Musical sounds – fill small boxes with rice, pulses, etc. to use as shakers

Goodies and baddies – 'cops and robbers', 'cowboys and indians', superheroes

Appendix 3: School day clock

With an older child they might draw their own clock face and draw the activities associated with each daytime hour. Have arrows point from the activity to the clock time that it mostly applies to.

Appendix 4: Transition calendar: Miffy's move

Table A.2

Monday	Tuesday	Wednesday	Thursday	Friday	Saturday	Sunday
Miffy meets her new parents	New parents take Miffy to park	Miffy visits new home, shown new room etc.	New parents visit Miffy at nursery	New parents put Miffy to bed	Miffy has pizza with new parents	Miffy's sleepover at her new home
Rest day Phone call for Miffy with new parents	New parents bring Miffy home for Tea	Review meeting	Farewell party at foster home	Day out with new parents	Parents collect Miffy from foster care to take her home	Miffy playing at new home Meets new granny
Social worker visits Miffy	Miffy goes to new nursery					

Appendix 5: Stories

Story 1 *Enry Elf*

Once upon a time in the woods, there were lots of elves and pixies. Most of them helped each other, but some argued a lot. Father Elf drank too much Foxglove wine. This made him angry. He gave some to Mother Elf and it made her sleepy. When she hadn't got his dinner ready, he lost his temper. The children hid from him but got hurt. Enry was scared. He tried to look after his mum but it was very hard. The other elves told Santa about Enry and his brothers and sisters' plight. Santa said, *'It's wrong to hurt children. And so near Christmas too!'* Of course, Santa was kind so he asked around to see who could help. Some pixies he knew said they would look after the young elves. Santa got his reindeers ready and took the children to the pixies' houses. Enry and his brothers and sisters went to different homes because there wasn't enough room in the pixies' toadstool homes to fit them all in under just one roof.

Mother Pixie showed Enry his new bed. She was kind but he found everything so different. Enry was scared he'd forget what to do or lose his way. He had to keep asking and it was really tiring. At times the pixies got fed up with all his questions.

Mother Pixie was busy getting things ready for Christmas and asked Enry to look for acorns. He said, *'Yes'* but by the time he got outside he'd forgotten what she'd asked him to do. Enry wailed, *'I can't do anything right!'* Luckily one of Santa's helpers heard him and told Santa that Enry was sounding worried and upset. Santa arranged for Enry to see his brothers and sisters. Santa asked each elf and pixie to suggest a game they could all play and food they liked. The helpers made a list and the mother pixies brought the elves' favourite snacks along. Everyone had a lovely time. When they got home, Mother Pixie made a calendar for Enry. It showed photos and pictures of events planned for Christmas so Enry would know what would happen and when. Enry stopped panicking now he knew what to expect. He looked forward to eating Mrs Pixie's pumpkin pie and playing games he knew.

Story 2 *Hopscotch*

Once upon a time a young bunny was feeling
very sad. You see, Mummy bunny had left her
with some hares to look after her. Wise Owl
heard about it and found a family of rabbits
to look after the young bunny. It was a big
family, who bunny liked, but all of a sudden
several of them left home. The bunny was
upset because now she had lost even more
people she had come to like.

The grown-up rabbits felt sad to see the young bunny so unhappy. Then Mummy
Rabbit had a bright idea. She said, *'Let's play hopscotch!'* Well, bunnies are very good
at hopping, so this made the young bunny very happy. They played hopscotch every
day, and the little bunny grew to love her new family very much.

Story 3 *A Brave Kitten Called Jingle*

When Jingle was born, Mummy Cat was very happy. She loved
her kitten's pretty eyes and licked him all over. The cats lived in
a back yard where lots of rubbish piled up. Most days Mummy
Cat went off on the prowl and met other tomcats – she enjoyed
parties and singing as cats do. But there were dangers in their
alley. Sometimes rats from the sewers joined them. Then
snakes came along and gave them snake juice. It made Mummy
Cat happy at first, but tired and sick later. She kept forgetting
about her kitten. Jingle rode on milk floats hoping for milk.

He searched in dustbins and cut his paws on tins. He followed
Mummy Cat into the sewers and got covered in muck. Insects stuck to his fur and
made him feel quite sick. Mummy Cat met another alley cat, and before long Jingle
had a sister kitten. But she carried on partying because she enjoyed it so much and
loved the snake juice as well. Lots of cats fought in the alley. Mummy Cat wasn't very
good at knowing which cats she could trust. Now he had a baby sister, Jingle went
looking for food for both of them. At night the kittens were cold and wet. They mewed
all night long. Fed up, Mummy Cat gave them snake juice to keep them quiet. One day
a kind lady heard the kittens crying and was very sad to see the mess they were in.
She took them to a Cat Home then went back to Mummy Cat and told her *'Go to the
Animal Sanctuary and learn how to be a good mother!'* But Mummy Cat didn't go. The
kind lady was worried and told Wise Owl about the kittens. He decided they needed
a kind family to look after them properly. The lady found a kind family of marmalade

cats for the kittens to live with. Jingle still worried about Mummy Cat but was happy now that he could play all day long. He liked feeling safe and warm and not having to look for food.

Story 4 *The Star that Lost its Shine*

Once upon a time, a bright star in the sky was stuck in a dark cloud full of chilly raindrops. The star couldn't find a way out and thought sadly, *'I've lost my shine!'* The moon couldn't see the star and wondered where she'd gone. The bright star was worried because she knew there were ships that wanted her light to guide them into the harbour, but she was well and truly stuck. Clouds gathered and lightning flashed across the sky. Waves crashed against the shore and harbour wall. People on the ships were scared. No one knew what to do on this darkest of nights as the rain poured in torrents. Suddenly, the star dropped into the ocean, feeling very scared indeed.

Just then a fisherman cast his net. Seeing the star caught in it, the fisherman grasped his rope and threw it to the hooks on the quayside. He fastened his boat and released the star from his net. *'Thank you'* said the star. As the star rose into the sky, Mother Nature got the clouds to part and said to the star, *'Thank goodness you are back where you belong! We need your light!'* The little star shone brightly and said *'From now on I shall take care of myself!'* The Moon agreed to help the star keep out of the rain clouds. The star shone ever more brightly from that time on!

Story 5 *The Brave Warrior*

Once upon a time, in an empire among the stars, fierce battles raged between evil guys and good people. Some of the planets were swampy and smelly, infested with creepy crawlies. Jonny Star had left his auntie and uncle on one of these swampy planets. He had found out that Auntie was actually his mum, but he didn't believe it. Most of the time, Auntie smelled vile and wobbled unsteadily. Both she and his uncle had been really mean to him. They made him do everything, treating him as a slave. Jonny kept wondering who his real dad was. He met a Dark Wizard who was head of the baddies, and who told Jonny, *'I am your father! Come with me!'* He wanted Jonny on his team.

Jonny knew the Dark Wizard was a bad guy who'd captured Princess Lucy. She had been trying to look after people whose homes were destroyed. A kind knight told Jonny *'Princess Lucy is your sister. Your real dad is Arras Star.'* Jonny decided to fight the evil guys. He made friends with some robots, who gave him a light sabre then he told the Sky Police to make lightning. Jonny won the battle and was about to kill the Dark Wizard but then he thought, *'That will only make me as bad as he is'*, so he didn't. It turned out that the he Dark Wizard was Arras Star all along but Jonny wasn't sure. He took the mask off his father's face and saw in his eyes that his Dad still had some good in his heart.

The battles were not over yet. The Dark Wizard told the Emperor that Princess Lucy was plotting against him. They captured her and kept her prisoner on the Dark Wizard's space ship. Jonny asked his mate for help. They crept onto the space ship and rescued her. Jonny made a jewel-encrusted light sabre. He was ready when the evil guys came for him.

Jonny leaped into a chasm and found himself in a deep hole. The horrible stink reminded him of his aunt and uncle, who screamed at him and blamed him for everything that went wrong. He felt glad he'd got away from them. Eventually, Jonny climbed out of the hole and leapt onto a boat, gripping the mast for dear life, scared he'd fall and drown or get killed. Luckily Princess Lucy was passing by on her ship and spotted him. She turned the ship round as quickly as she could and rescued him. *'Thanks!'* said Jonny. *'You are the bravest hero I've ever met!'* said Princess Lucy.

She and Jonny got all the good people in the empire together and they sent the Dark Wizard to a different universe. Others were warned that they'd be sent there too if they didn't follow the good people's rules. Luckily most of them did. So Jonny and Princess Lucy lived in peace from that time on.

Glossary of terms

Affect   The noun 'affect' refers to the outward expression of emotions.

Arousal-relaxation cycle   In this cycle, the infant expresses a need that the nurturing parent meets, enabling the infant to relax in the expectation that the cycle will repeat.

Attunement   This refers to tuning in to another's feelings and showing empathy without being overwhelmed by the feelings that are being projected.

Attachment   Attachment theory explains how young children organise their behaviour to secure the attention of their primary caregivers in order to survive. When first-time mothers look at their infants' faces, the reward areas of their brains 'light up' (Strathearn et al., 2009). These attachment relationships can also develop between infants and non-maternal caregivers – fathers, grandparents, foster and adoptive parents and child care workers. As babies express their feelings (such as hunger or discomfort), they learn to respond in ways that secure their survival (Panksepp, 2012). Neglected children who do not experience this early on will struggle later. Children who show insecure attachment may become 'avoidant' (to protect themselves from parents' displeasure) or resistant/ambivalent (to maintain attention via confrontational and clingy or risky behaviour). If neither strategy works, the child may swing between the extreme patterns of avoidance and aggression associated with 'disorganised' attachment (Main, 2000) – see Chapter 3.

Bonding   This refers to bonds formed from growing affection between parent and child.

Cause and effect   Nurtured children learn in the first year of life that actions have consequences. The more repeatedly this occurs the more they can predict a response, for example, the child in his highchair might drop a toy to see what happens – '*Will it come back?*' Inevitably the object doesn't return of its own volition. The child may cry in disappointment but the nurturing parent returns the toy to the child, who throws it again. The child realises that, '*I throw, mummy returns it to me therefore I am worthy of attention!*' By contrast, the children of unresponsive parents learn the opposite message (that they are unwanted and ineffectual) so tend to be slower to discover the effect their actions have on others around them.

Dissociation   When a child experiences a threat such as repeated sexual and physical abuse that is utterly overwhelming and too much for their fight / flight

Glossary of terms

system to cope with, she may have the sense of being a 'fly on the wall' watching what is happening from outside herself, as her brain goes into a 'freeze' state of numbing or collapse. The child experiences this sort of trauma as a general shutdown, shows lack of vitality and often presents as emotionally detached.

Empathy   Empathy is the ability to recognise another's feelings and respond to them appropriately (Baron-Cohen, 1985). Children learn empathy from having it modelled to them. Children in care and adopted are especially dependent on caregiving parents to train them how to 'step into another's shoes', 'see through another's eyes' to recognise others' feelings in order to respond reciprocally.

Hypervigilance   The most commonly recognised symptom of trauma, hypervigilance is a heightened state of awareness that is part of the fight / flight response. It is akin to being locked into permanent 'battle stations'; brain resources are on constant alert, causing inappropriate and sometimes aggressive reactions in everyday situations. It is accompanied by an exaggerated intensity of behaviours whose purpose is to keep close watch. However, it raises anxiety and causes exhaustion for both the child and caregiver. The child is constantly scanning their environment in search of sights, sounds, people, behaviours, smells, or anything else that is reminiscent of traumatic threat. He is on high alert to ensure that danger is not near. Hypervigilance can lead to a variety of obsessive behaviour patterns, as well as difficulties with sleep, social interaction and relationships.

Magical thinking   Pre-school age children will be at the stage of 'magical thinking' which means they assume they have all sorts of powers to make things happen, for example, make the people on TV talk to them. The anxious child might think his ill wishes cause bad things to happen, such as his caregivers getting ill.

Mentalisation   This is the ability to understand one's own mental state and that of others, including children. It helps us make sense of our thoughts, wishes and feelings and how these affect our actions and behaviour.

Mind-mindedness   This is a parenting approach that assumes even very young children have independent thoughts and feelings. Parents making emotionally appropriate responses to their child's expressions of feeling is a predictor of attachment security and theory of mind – the ability to understand that other's thoughts and feelings may differ to theirs.

Mirroring   In the context of this book, mirroring is the copying and reflecting of another's behaviour, including facial and body expressions, tone and eye movements, usually in interaction between the caregiving parent and child.

Neuroscience   This refers to research emanating from study of the brain. Neuroscience is the study of the brain's nervous system and the way it functions. It is used to help us understand key issues in early childhood development. This is because continuous exposure to traumatic incidents, including neglect, has a powerful and deleterious effect on brain development. Emotional health is essential to learning and cognition. The brain is hypersensitive to environmental experience in early childhood while it is growing at its fastest rate during the first five years of life.

Object permanence   This is the recognition that people or things exist even when they are hidden from view. The child learns it in the course of exploration. On repeatedly finding objects placed out of sight, the child realises that even when she can't see it, it will still be there somewhere. Fraiberg (2006) advises that if the object is moved to a different place, the child will initially look in the original place but within a few weeks she learns that with persistence she will find it. This concept of an objective world facilitates children's rational thought processing.

Play therapy   Play therapy developed from the recognition that before children develop sophisticated use of language to express themselves, they express their thoughts and feelings adroitly through play, which can be used to treat children with psychological problems.. The British Association of Play Therapists define play therapy as '*a way of helping children express their feelings and deal with their emotional problems, using play as the main communication tool*'.

Post-traumatic stress disorder (PTSD)   Children who experience repeated trauma as the consequence of subjection to serious neglect and abuse can develop PTSD. Symptoms of PTSD typically include hypervigilance, sleep disturbance with nightmares and night terrors, appetite loss, enuresis and encopresis.

Reflective functioning   This is a parenting theory developed by Peter Fonagy et al (2002). Reflective functioning allows parents and caregivers to understand behaviour and communicate mental states. This enables them to teach children how to regulate their behaviour by reflecting on feelings. Such communication also enhances the child's cognitive development.

Resilience   Resilience is the capacity to recover quickly from difficulties. Research has shown that for looked after children, the ability to recover from adversity becomes far more difficult when neglect has compromised their development. Without high quality care to compensate for early neglect, they are likely to underachieve in many domains and to suffer anxiety and mental ill health. Education as well as caregiving has an important role in promoting resilience.

Sculpting   Sculpting is a dramatherapeutic device for projecting emotional states and situations. It can involve making arrangements of pieces, such as toy figures, or buttons, to show relationships. In dramatic play, it involves bending other players' bodies into a shape to project an emotion and an aspect of the relationships between them.

Self-regulation   This is the ability to control one's emotions. It is an important development that allows children to manage their feelings, behaviour and body movements, so they can pay attention and stay focussed in the face of stressful situations.

Glossary of terms

Sensory integration   In order to deal with and respond to incoming stimuli the brain needs to be able to integrate information from the five senses – hearing, sight, smell, touch and taste – as well as those of interoception, proprioception, and the vestibular system. Interoception is the sense of the internal state of the body and may be conscious or unconscious. The brain integrates signals from the body, enabling self-awareness. Proprioception refers to the group of muscles that enable us to control physical movements. The vestibular system is for balance and coordination. Neglect and trauma interfere with this development. Consequently, the affected child may not recognise their body temperature, for example, and may have poor balance or coordination. Sometimes the body's nervous system, especially in young children, is unable to integrate sensory information due to sensory overload and it becomes overexcited or overwhelmed.

Separation anxiety   This is about children's anxiety on being separated from a parent, often expressed through the child clinging on and crying. It is common and normal in children from one to three years, after which many grow out of it. For some children who have experienced their parent to be unreliable (they may have promised to be back in a minute then disappear for hours), separation anxiety can persist and transfer to new carers due to the child's underlying fear of being abandoned. It leaves the child ever watchful and unable to risk leaving the parent's side to play or try out a new activity.

Transitional object   Psychologist Donald Winnicott (1953) saw children dealing with temporary separation from their parents by holding on to a favourite soft toy or cloth, which he described as a transitional object. This item often retained the smell of the parent and served as a representation of her. Moves in care mean that fostered and adopted children may not have kept their significant objects. Giving the child something of the carer's to look after communicates that the carer will reappear eventually to retrieve the object and reassures the child.

Trauma   Where adopted and fostered children are concerned, trauma refers to the experience of traumatic events that cause extreme stress which overwhelms the affected child's ability to cope and delays their recovery. Traumatic memories can be inadvertently set in motion by the scent or facial expression of a person (regardless of the person's intentions). Research shows that such memories become harder to alter, since 'states become traits' (Robert-Tissot et al, 1996). Traumatised children are easily overwhelmed by feelings of shame, fear, embarrassment, and anger when triggered unconsciously by memories of past trauma that cause them to feel inadequate or less than perfect

Visceral   These are feelings felt deep down inside the body, e.g. in the heart, liver and intestines. Based on instinct and intuition rather than intellect and thought, these feelings are felt very deeply, and are difficult to control.

References

Alexander, L. (1986) *Scared of the Dark*. USA: Sesame Street Productions

Baillargeon R. (1987) Object permanence in 3½- and 4½-month-old infants. *Developmental Psychology* 23, 655–664.

Baillargeon R. (1991) Reasoning about the height and location of a hidden object in 4.5- and 6.5-month-old infants. *Cognition* 38, 13–42.

Baron-Cohen S., Leslie A.M., Frith U. (1985) Does the autistic child have a theory of mind? *Cognition* 21, 37–46.

Banks J. and Xu X. (2020) *The mental health effects of the first two months of lockdown and social distancing during the COVID-19 pandemic in the UK*. Institute for Fiscal Studies working paper W20/16. London: Econstor.

Bercow J. (2008) *The Bercow Report: a review of services for children and young people (0–19) with speech, language and communication needs.* Department for Education.

Blackmore J., Burns G., Waters C.S. and Shelton K.H. (2020) 'The very first thing that connected us to him': Adopters' experiences of sharing photographs, 'talking' albums and other materials with their children prior to meeting them. *Adoption and Fostering* 44(3), 225–241.

Booth Church E., (2021) Teaching *techniques: Resolving conflicts*. Available at: www.scholastic.com/teachers/articles/teaching-content/teaching-techniques-resolving-conflicts/

Bowlby J. (1973) *The Making and Breaking of Affectional Bonds*, 2nd edn. London: Routledge.

Branden M., Glaser D., Maquire S., McRory E., Lushey C., Ward H. (2014) *Missed Opportunities: Indicators of neglect – what is ignored, why and what can be done?* Research report. Department for Education.

Bunstan W., Eyre K., Carlsonn A., Pringle K. (2016) Evaluating relational repair work with infants and mothers impacted by family violence. *Australia and New Zealand Journal of Criminology* 49(1), 113–133.

Bunston W. and Jones S.J. (eds) (2020) *Supporting Vulnerable Babies and Young Children: Interventions for Working with Trauma, Mental Health, Illness and Other Complex Challenges*. London: Jessica Kingsley.

References

Caspi A., Houts R.M., Belsky D.W., Harrington H., Hogan S., Ramrakha S., Poulton R. and Moffit T.E. (2016) Childhood forecasting of a small section of the population with a large economic burden. *Nature Human Behaviour* 1. Available at: www.nature.com/articles/s41562-016-0005

Clarke, R., Menna R., McAndrew, A J., Johnson E M. (2020) Language, aggression and self-regulation in young children. *Journal of Emotional and Behavioural Disorders* https://doi.org/10.1177%2F1063426620937691

Corrigan M. and Moore J. (2011) *Listening to Children's Wishes and Feelings, Training and handbook,* London: BAAF.

Department for Education (2020) Early Years Foundation Stage Statutory Framework, Standard and Testing agency. Available at: www.gov.uk/government/publications/early-years-foundation-stage-framework--2#history

Department for Education (2020) Statistics: looked after children. Statistics on children under local authority care at national and local authority level. Available at: https://explore-education-statistics.service.gov.uk/find-statistics/children-looked-after-in-england-including-adoptions/2020

Department for Education (2020) *Ofsted Annual Report 2019/2020: Education, children's services and skills.* Available at: www.gov.uk/government/publications/ofsted-annual-report-201920-education-childrens-services-and-skills

Dozier M., Higley E., Albus K.E., and Nutter A. (2002) Intervening with foster infants' caregivers: Targeting three critical needs. *Infant Mental Health Journal* 23(5), 541–554.

Erikson E. (1950) *Childhood and Society.* Stanford: W. W. Norton

Eyre K., Milburn N. and Bunstan W. (2020) 'Murder in their family': Making space for experience of the infant impacted by familial murder. In: Bunston W. and Jones S.J. (eds) *Supporting Vulnerable Babies and Young Children: Interventions for Working with Trauma, Mental Health, Illness and Other Complex Challenges.* London: Jessica Kingsley, pp. 107–123.

Fahlberg V. (1994) *A Child's Journey Through Placement.* London: BAAF.

Faulconbridge J., Hunt, K., Laffan A., Fatimilehin I., Law D. (eds.) (2018) *Improving the Psychological Wellbeing of children and young people.* London: Jessica Kingsley

Figley C.R. (ed.) (1995) *Compassion Fatigue: Coping with Secondary Traumatic Stress Disorder in Those Who Treat the Traumatised.* New York: Brunner/Mazel.

Fonagy P., Gergely G., Jurist E.L. and Target M. (2002) *Affect Regulation, Mentalisation and the Development of Self.* New York: Other Press.

Fonagy P. and Target M. (2006) The mentalization-based approach to self-pathology. *Journal of Personality Disorders* 20, 544–576.

Fraiberg S. (2006) *The Magic Years: Understanding and Handling the Problems of Early Childhood.* New York: Simon & Schuster.

Frude N. and Killick S. (2011). Family storytelling and the attachment relationship. *Psychodynamic Practice* 17, 441–455.

Gerhardt S. (2004) *Why Love Matters: How Affection Shapes the Baby's Brain.* London: Taylor & Francis.

Hambrick E., Brawner T., and Perry (2018) Examining developmental diversity and connectedness in child welfare-involved children. *Children Australia* 43(2), 105–115.

Hashmi S., Vanderwert R.E., Price H.A., Gerson S.A. (2020) Exploring the benefits of doll play through neuroscience. *Frontiers in Human Neuroscience* 14, 560176 https://doi.org/10.3389/fnhum.2020.560176

Hendry D. and Chapman J. (1999) *The Very Noisy Night*, London: Little Tiger Press.

Howe D. (2005) *Child Abuse and Neglect: Attachment Development and Intervention.* Basingstoke: Palgrave Macmillan.

Hughes D. (2004) An attachment-based treatment of maltreated children and young people. *Attachment & Human Development* 6, 263–278.

Hughes D. (2017) Finding our way to reciprocity: Working with children who find it difficult to trust. In: Daniel S. and Trevarthen C. (eds) *Rhythms of Relating in Children's Therapies.* London: Jessica Kingsley, pp. 113–125.

Hughes J.I. (2020) Twenty years since the MacPherson report. How much do Black children's lives matter in the UK? *Seen and Heard* 30(3), 66–70.

Jenney A. (2020) Keeping the child in mind when thinking about violence in families. In: Bunston W. and Jones S.J. (eds) *Supporting Vulnerable Babies and Young Children: Interventions for Working with Trauma, Mental Health, Illness and Other Complex Challenges.* London: Jessica Kingsley, pp. 91–106.

Jennings S. (2004) *Creative Storytelling with Children at Risk.* Bicester: Speechmark

References

Keenan T. and Evans S. (2009) *An Introduction to Child Development*. London: Sage.

Kenrick J., Lindsey C. and Tollemache L. (Eds) (2019) *Creating New Families: Therapeutic Approaches to Fostering, Adoption and Kinship Care*. Abingdon: Routledge.

Killick S. (2014) 'A play on words': Helping foster carers build attachments and create meaning through storytelling. *Child & Family Clinical Psychology Review* 2. The British Psychological Society.

Kim S. and Strathearn L. (2014) Mothers who are securely attached in pregnancy show more attuned infant mirroring 7 months postpartum. *Infant Behavior and Development* 37(4), 491–504.

Laming L. (2003) *The Victoria Climbie Inquiry*. Norwich: HMSO.

Laming L. (2009) *The Protection of Children in England: A Progress Report.* London: The Stationery Office.

Lanyado M. (2003) The emotional tasks of moving from fostering to adoption: Transitions, attachment, separation and loss. *Clinical Child Psychology and Psychiatry* 8(3), 337–349.

Lieberman A.E., Ghosh Ippen C., and Van Horn P. (2015) *Don't Hit My Mommy! A Manual for Child-Parent Psychotherapy with Young Children Exposed to Violence and Other Trauma* (2nd edn). Washington DC: Zero-Three.

Lindsey C. and Kenrick J. (2019) *Creating New Families: Therapeutic Approaches to Fostering, Adoption and Kinship Care*. Abingdon: Routledge.

Lindsey G. and Dockrell J. (2012) *The Relationship Between Speech, Language and Communication Needs and Behavioural Emotional and Social Difficulties*. Better Communication Research Programme. London: Department for Education.

Lloyd S. (2016) *Improving Sensory Processing in Traumatised Children.* London: Jessica Kingsley.

Rogers M. (2013) *Daniel Pelka Serious Case Review*. Coventry Local Safeguarding Children Board. Children's Services Network Policy Briefing, 2 October.

Main M. (2000) The organised strategies of infant, child and adult attachment: Flexible versus inflexible attention under attachment-related stress. *Journal of the American Psychoanalytic Association* 48, 1055–1095.

Maslow A. (1970) *Motivation and Personality.* New York: Harper and Row.

Mayer M. (1991) *There's a Nightmare in my Cupboard.* London: Moonlight Publishing Ltd.

McFie J., Cicchetti D., Toth S.L. (2001) The development of dissociation in maltreated pre-school children. *Development and Psychopathology* 13(2), 233–254.

Moore J. (2012) *Once-Upon-A-Time Stories and Drama to Use in Direct Work with Adopted and Fostered Children.* London: BAAF.

Moore J. (2014) *Emotional Problem Solving Using Stories, Drama and Play.* Buckingham: Hinton House.

Moore J. (2019) 'The Storying Spiral': a narrative-dramatic approach to life story therapy with adoptive/foster families and traumatised children. *International Journal of Play* 8(3), 204–218.

Moore J. (2020) *Narrative and Dramatic Approaches to Children's Life Story with Foster, Adoptive and Kinship Families.* London: Routledge.

Music G. (2014) *The Good Life: Wellbeing and the New Science of Altruism, Selfishness and Immorality.* Hove: Routledge.

Music G. (2020) Foreword. In: Bunstan W. and Jones S.J. (eds) *Supporting Vulnerable Babies and Young Children: Interventions for Working with Trauma, Mental Health, Illness and Other Complex Challenges.* London: Jessica Kingsley, pp. 7–10.

Naughton A., Maguire S., Mann M., Lumn C., Tempest V., Gracias S., and Kemp A. (2013) Emotional, behavioural and developmental features indicative of neglect or emotional abuse in pre-school children: A systematic review. *JAMA Pediatrics* 167(8), 769–775.

Norris V. and Rodwell H. (2017) *Parenting with Theraplay: Understanding Attachment and How to Nurture a Closer Relationship with Your Child.* London: Jessica Kingsley.

O'Connor A. (2018) *Understanding Transition in the Early Years: Supporting Change Through Attachment and Resilience,* 2nd edn. Abingdon: Routledge.

Ogendele M. (2020) Profile of neurodevelopmental and behavioural problems and associated psychosocial factors among a cohort of newly looked after children in an English local authority. *Adoption and Fostering* 44(3), 255–271.

Padilla J.B., Vargas J.H., and Chavez L. (2010) Influence of age on transracial foster adoptions and its relation to ethnic identity development. *Adoption Quarterly* 13(1), 50–73.

Panksepp J. and Biven L. (2012) *The Archaeology of Mind: Neuroevolutionary Origins of Human Emotions.* London and New York: Norton.

References

Pascal C., Bertram T., Ceillinane C., Hold-White E. (2020) *COVID-19 and Social Mobility, Impact Brief 4: Early Years*, The Sutton Trust, July issue. Available at: www.suttontrust.com/wp-content/uploads/2020/06/Early-Years-Impact-Brief.pdf

Patterson J.M. (2002) Understanding family resilience. *Journal of Clinical Psychology* 58, 233–246.

Perry B., Pollard R., Blakely T., Baker W., & Vigilante D. (1995) Childhood trauma, the neurobiology of adaptation and 'use dependent' development of the brain: How 'states' become 'traits'. *Infant Mental Health Journal* 16(4), 271–191.

Perry B. (2002) Childhood experience and the expression of genetic potential: What childhood tells us about nature and nurture. *Brain and Mind* 3, 79–100.

Perry B.D., Anda R.F., Felitti V.J., Bremner J.D., Walker J.D., Whitfield C.H. (2006) The enduring effects of abuse and related adverse experiences in childhood. *European Archives of Psychiatry and Clinical Neuroscience* 256(3), 174–186.

Petrakopoulou A. (2011) The use of aggressive-release toys in non-directive play therapy: Is there any impact on children's aggressive behaviour? *British Journal of Play Therapy* 7, 58–73.

Pfister M. (1997) *Milo and the Magical Stones*. London: North-South Books.

Piaget J. (1952) *The Origins of Intelligence in Children*. New York: International University Press.

Porges S. and Daniel S. (2017) Play and the dynamics of treating medical trauma: Insights from polyvagal theory. In: Daniel S. and Trevarthen C. (eds) *Rhythms of Relating in Children's Therapies*. London: Jessica Kingsley, pp. 113–125.

Robert-Tissot C., Cramer B., Stern D.N., Rusconi Serpa S., Bachmann J.-P., Palacio Espasa F., et al. (1996) Mother–Infant Psychotherapies: Report on 75 Cases. *Infant Mental Health Journal* 17(2), 97-114.

Schechter D.S., Coates S.W., Kaminer T., Coots T. et al (2008) Distorted maternal mental representations and atypical behaviour in a clinical sample of violence-exposed mother and their toddlers. *Journal of Trauma and Dissociation* 9(2), 123–147.

Schore A. (2006) *Affect Regulation and Disorders of the Self*. New York: Norton

Schore, A. and Sieff D. F. (2015) On the same wavelength: how our human brain is shaped by human relationships. In: Sieff, D.F. (ed.) *Understanding and Healing Emotional Trauma: Conversations with Pioneering Clinicians and Researchers*. Abingdon: Routledge, pp. 111-136

Selwyn J., Meakings S., and Wijedasa D. (2014) *Beyond the Adoption Order: Challenges, Intervention, Disruption*. London: BAAF.

Sigley I. (2020) 'It has touched us all': Commenting on the social implications of touch during the COVID-19 pandemic. *Social Sciences and Humanities Open Journal* 2(1), 100051.

Stern D.N. (1985) *The Interpersonal World of the Infant*. New York: Basic Books.

Strathearn L., Fonagy P., Amico J., and Montague P.R. (2009) Adult attachment predicts maternal brain and oxytocin response to infant cues. *Neuropsychopharmacology* 34, 2655–2666.

Struik A. (2019) *Treating Chronically Traumatised Children: The Sleeping Dogs Method*. London: Routledge.

Thomas T. and Killick S. (2007) *Telling Tales: Storytelling as Emotional Literacy*. Blackburn: Educational Printing Services.

Thomson R. (2020) 5 things you need to know about...'object permanence'. *Nursery World*, Issue 10, 2 July. Available at: www.magonlinelibrary.com/toc/nuwa/current

Townsend M. (2020) Revealed: Surge in domestic violence during COVID-19 crisis. *Observer*, 12 April. Available at: www.theguardian.com/society/2020/apr/12/domestic-violence-surges-seven-hundred-per-cent-uk-coronavirus

Trevarthen C. (2005) First things first: Infants make good use of the sympathetic rhythm of imitation without reason or language. *Journal of Child Psychotherapy* 31, 91–113.

Trevarthen C., and Aitken K.J. (1994) Brain development, infant communication, and empathy disorders: Intrinsic factors in child mental health. *Developmental Psychopathology* 6, 599–635.

Triseliotis J. (2002) Long-term foster care or adoption? The evidence examined. *Child and Family Social Work* 7(1), 23–33.

Tronick, E., Adamson, L.B., Als, H., and Brazelton, T.B. (1975). *Infant emotions in normal and perturbated interactions*. Paper presented at the biennial meeting of the Society for Research in Child Development, Denver, CO. Available at: https://blogs.scientificamerican.com/thoughtful-animal/ed-tronick-and-the-8220-still-face-experiment-8221/

Urbina-Garcia A. (2020) *Young children's mental health: Impact of social isolation during the COVID-19 lockdown and effective strategies*. Available at: https://hull-repository.worktribe.com/output/3693454

References

Van der Kolk B. (2015) *The Body Keeps the Score: Mind, Brain and Body in the Transformation of Trauma*. London: Penguin.

Vygotsky L. (1978) *Mind and Society: The Development of Higher Mental Processes*. Cambridge, MA: Harvard University Press.

Wakelyn J. (2020) Developing an intervention for infants and young children in foster care. In: Bunston W. and Jones S.J. (eds) *Supporting Vulnerable Babies and Young Children: Interventions for Working with Trauma, Mental Health, Illness and Other Complex Challenges*. London: Jessica Kingsley, pp. 74–87.

Weber C. and Haen A. (2005) *Clinical Applications of Drama Therapy in Child and Adolescent Treatment*. Hove: Brunner-Routledge.

Winnicott D. (1953) Transitional objects and transitional phenomena: A study of the first not-me possession, part 1. *International Journal of Psycho-Analysis* 34, 89-97

Winnicott D. (1971) *Playing and Reality*. London: Tavistock/Routledge.

Winnicott D. (1965) *Maturational Processes and the Facilitating Environment: Studies in the Theory of Emotional Development*. London: Hogarth Press.

Index

Index

Index

Index